James Marchant

Theories of the Resurrection of Jesus Christ

James Marchant

Theories of the Resurrection of Jesus Christ

ISBN/EAN: 9783744648462

Printed in Europe, USA, Canada, Australia, Japan

Cover: Foto ©Lupo / pixelio.de

More available books at **www.hansebooks.com**

THEORIES
OF THE RESURRECTION OF
JESUS CHRIST.

BY

JAMES MARCHANT

*(Sometime Evidential Lecturer to the Barking Rural Deaneries
and the Christian Evidence Society).*

WILLIAMS AND NORGATE,

14, HENRIETTA STREET, COVENT GARDEN, LONDON.

20, SOUTH FREDERICK STREET, EDINBURGH,

AND 7, BROAD STREET, OXFORD.

1899.

FOREWORD.

THIS little book is unhappily not behind the times. Non-supernatural theories of the Resurrection of Jesus Christ are not yet dead. It may be true, as Schaff says, that they are " standing jokes " in the fashionable circles of Germany, but it is not true that they are jokes amongst more serious if, in some respects, less educated people.

At one time these theories may have influenced fashionable circles only, now they are openly discussed in weekly sceptical newspapers, in cheap pamphlets assiduously circulated, by lectures in public halls and open spaces in cities, towns and villages, to hundreds and sometimes to several thousands of persons. The writer has constantly read these papers, heard these lectures, spoken to these congregations, and for some years it was his daily and often heart-breaking duty to try to clear away these theories from the minds of men and women, young and old. To them, these theories were serious obstacles to faith in Jesus Christ, and still are so to many who remain in doubt.

The swoon theory may be a century old, but it is advocated in England by at least one learned clergyman, to an intelligent West-end congregation, to this hour.

The vision theory is defended from one well-known London pulpit by two eminent preachers.

The modification of the vision theory, which, in this book, is called the apparition theory, is, in Spiritualistic circles (which, since the strange conversion of Mrs. Besant to Theosophy, have temporarily widened), *the* theory of the hour.

The theory of conspiracy will be entirely novel to many readers. It is here, for the first time, quoted and examined, so far as it deserves examination. This theory, unlike the others, is not of German manufacture ; it was made in England, and in England alone is it advocated. That is our honour.

It is not these theories as theories, however, that we are exclusively concerned to combat. It is the objections urged in support of these theories which exercise a subtle influence over the minds of many people. The scanty reference to some objections which, under other circumstances, would have demanded more detailed examination, the slight construction of the chapters, the footnotes and copious references, have been written throughout with the results of that influence in the writer's mind. Apart from these grievous results, and the fact that some of the objections are seriously stated by writers who enjoy the daily confidence of their readers, they are not worthy of an answer.

And how many Christians, alas! live in the shadow of a threatening doubt which makes glad and perfect faith in Jesus Christ almost impossible. The writer has listened to many whose story would have made the hearts of their ministers bleed had it ever reached their ears. The memory of these never-to-be-forgotten conversations and lectures and meetings is linked by loving ties to this little book.

It will not be urged by those who take a practical interest in helping doubters that a book like this is not needed. And because there is not one written in a popular way, and published at a price within the reach of persons who have not the time to read or the money to buy the critical works of eminent writers upon the subject, this one has been undertaken in the midst of many duties by one who has one qualification—he has lived amongst rational-ists, and has himself passed under the black cloud of intellectual doubt. He has felt the unspeakable wretchedness of the soul when faith in the Redeemer has been lost, and now for ten years he has known the inexpressible joys of regaining it.

"Happy is the man," he would say, in the words of Archbishop Trench, " and he only is happy, who, if the outworks of his faith are at any time assailed, can betake himself to an impregnable inner citadel, from whence in due time to issue forth and repossess even those exterior defences, who can fall back on those inner grounds of belief in which there can be no mistake, the testimony of the Spirit, which is above and better than all."

The Manse, Canonbury, N.

1899.

CONTENTS.

CHAPTER I

SPIRITUAL EVIDENCE.

CHAPTER II

THE TESTIMONY OF THE EVANGELISTS.

CONTENTS.

CHAPTER III

THE SWOON THEORY.

CHAPTER IV

VISION AND APPARITION THEORIES.

CONTENTS.

CHAPTER V

THE THEORY OF CONSPIRACY.

CHAPTER VI

SOME THEORETICAL OBJECTIONS.

To All who Doubt
The Resurrection of Jesus Christ
from the Dead
This Little Volume
is Inscribed by
The Author.

SPIRITUAL EVIDENCE.

"He is not risen!" Think if some angel voice, trumpet-tongued, proclaimed from Heaven this new message—Gospel I may not call it—to the awe-stricken world. To those who dwell at ease, to those whose life is joyous, they might seem words of little meaning; but what to the weary and aged, what to the way-worn farers on the path of life—that path strewn with flowers for a few but so flinty to many; what to the lonesome heart, which passes here longing for a love which may not be won, for some ideal, be it what it may, which can never be attained; what to the mother hungering for her child, and the orphan wailing for its parent; what to the wife bereft of her husband, or the strong man sorrow-stricken for the last joy of his life; what, in a word, will it be when we can hear no more by the open grave, "I am the Resurrection and the Life"? Gone are the hopes of meeting no more to part; gone is the vision of the golden city, where sin and sorrow cannot enter. Gone, in one word, all that has nerved souls of saints and assuaged the burden of sorrow for many a century past." (Bonney's sermon on "The Place of the Resurrection in Christianity.")

I

SPIRITUAL EVIDENCE.[1]

THE legal or historical evidence of the bare fact of the Resurrection of Jesus Christ should not be given undue prominence in Christian apologetics. Unbelievers, unable to understand the spiritual nature of Christian doctrines assume that the writers of the New Testament Scriptures wrote upon the subject of the Resurrection merely to state its legal proof as an historical reality:—"the natural man (that is, the man whose perceptions do not extend beyond the limits of his intellect) receiveth not the things of the Spirit of God : for they are foolishness unto him ; neither can he know them, because they are spiritually discerned." Dr. Strauss, building upon this assumption, devotes a whole section of his "Life of Jesus" to pointing out the unsatisfactory

[1]This opening article was written for "The King's Own," in which it appeared in 1897. It is here reprinted (revised) by kind permission of the Editor.

nature of the Gospel accounts. He evidently thinks that Matthew, Mark, Luke, and John deliberately isolated the story of the Resurrection from other doctrines and facts, and as deliberately wrote to prove that it happened. He examines their (to him) inadequate and fragmentary statements separately, and, to his own satisfaction, succeeds in showing that what the writers saw and state, and what they omit to state, and, perhaps, did not see, makes their story too weak to command our mental assent. He gives undue prominence to the legal or historical evidence of the Resurrection.

The Evangelists do not commit so grave an error. They do not obscure and distort the fair proportions of the glorious Gospel of Jesus Christ. Now the first requisite to a proper appreciation of the evidence for this blessed event is surely to understand not merely the legal proof, but the position which the doctrine itself occupied, in their estimation and belief, in the Christian economy. Another requisite, equally important, if we would do the subject, the witnesses, and ourselves justice, is to consider the Evangelists, until the contrary is shown, sincere men. They believed what they recorded,

Look at the fact of the Resurrection, as a matter of history, through the eyes of the Evangelists. The first obvious point is that they do not say much about it. St. Matthew and St. Mark devote one brief chapter, and St. Luke forty-eight verses to the subject. In the two chapters in St. John's Gospel is also described a special circumstance relating to our Lord's appearances. It is a constant objection that the writers do not give sufficient details. "The Resurrection is a stupendous event," says Dr. Strauss and others, in effect, "and therefore we are entitled to have every circumstance fully related." With no apologies to the sceptic, it may be safely said that if every detail had been given he would be a sceptic still. Renan begins his investigation of Christianity with the declaration that a miracle has never happened. "At the bottom of all discussion on such matters is the question of the supernatural. . . . Now the question of the supernatural is determined to us with absolute certainty by this simple reason, that there is no room for belief in a thing of which the world can offer no experimental trace.[1] We do not believe in a miracle, just as we do not believe in dreams, in the devil, in sorcery, or in astrology. Have we any need to refute step by step the long reasonings of astrology? No."[2] From this standpoint he investigates the Resurrection, and his conclusions have no more value than the assumption with which he starts.[3] If we look at the Resurrection through the eyes of Renan, we cannot be persuaded, " though one (actually) rose from the dead."

The absence from the Gospels of an elaborate historical proof of the Resurrection is evidence that the writers did not think of it as a mere matter of history. The meagreness of the space given to the subject, as compared with other matters, is further evidence that, in their judgment, the Resurrection,

[1] And the author (Mr W. R. Cassels) of "Supernatural Religion" writes:—" The belief that a dead man rose from the dead and appeared to several persons alive is at once disposed of upon abstract grounds. The alleged occurrence is contrary to universal experience." And again, "Any explanation consistent with universal experience must be adopted rather than a belief which is contrary to it." Vol. iii., p. 622.

[2] *Vie de Jesus*, p. 13.

[3] "Saladin," a writer of modern sceptical pamphlets, says:—" It would be more probable that every living historian should wilfully lie than that the Resurrection should have taken place." (Did Jesus Christ rise from the Dead? p. 4.)

as a *past* event, was not so important as it apparently is to the modern sceptic.

The immediate and convincing evidence to the apostles that Christ had risen, was *not* that the soldier who pierced the heart of Jesus and knew that He was dead ; nor that Joseph and Nicodemus, who buried Him with the rich ; nor that the women who loved Him, and "beheld where He lay," could be produced to testify to His death and burial. It was *not* that armed soldiers paced to and fro in the beautiful garden to guard the sealed tomb lest they or other friends of Jesus might steal His sacred body, although these very soldiers, by their absurd story, became witnesses in favour of the Resurrection. It was *not* the empty tomb, nor the fact that angels declared He was risen, reminding them that He had said that "the Son of Man must be delivered into the hands of sinful men, and be crucified, and the third day rise again." This evidence they do give, but it was evidence of a higher and a personal character that convinced them. They spoke of a present and living Christ, not ot His *past* Resurrection. Christ is living, that is their saving message. They did not trouble themselves *how* He arose from the dead ; where He obtained the clothes to cover His nakedness; or who saw Him rise. The one palpable, life-giving, inspiring fact was that Christ was alive. The evidence, to them, of the Resurrection was their own spiritual transformation and the descent of the Holy Ghost. These poor, unlearned men, after the arrest and crucifixion, with bitter and pathetic disappointment, went back to their boats and their nets, to the garden and the workshop—"We trusted that it had been he which should have redeemed Israel." These same men, after they had seen the risen Christ, and conversed, and eaten, and drunk with Him, were "endued with power from on high." The evidence of the Resurrection was their manifestation of spiritual power. The lame man at the Beautiful Gate, upon whom Peter and John fastened their eyes, and commanded, in the name of Jesus Christ, to rise up and walk, was, to them, evidence of a Risen Saviour. *The apostles could not have cured this man if Christ had been holden or imprisoned by death.* The evidence of the Resurrection was the Day of Pentecost, and the three thousand souls who owned Him as their Lord and their God, "continuing daily with one accord in the temple, and breaking bread from house to

house, did eat their meat with gladness and single-
ness of heart, praising God, and having favour with
all the people."

The Resurrection received its just historical and
doctrinal proportions in the reply of St. Peter to
the question of the astonished Jews, who witnessed
this marvellous manifestation of spiritual power and
asked one another " What meaneth this?   Others
mocking said, These men are full of new wine.

" But Peter, standing up with the eleven, lifted
up his voice and said unto them, Ye men of Judæa,
and all ye that dwell at Jerusalem, be this known
unto you, and hearken to my words : For these
are not drunken, as ye suppose, seeing it is but the
third hour of the day.

" But this is that which was spoken by the
prophet Joel ; And it shall come to pass in the last
days, saith God, I will pour out of my Spirit upon
all flesh : and your sons and your daughters shall
prophesy, and your young men shall see visions,
and your old men shall dream dreams : And on my
servants and on my handmaidens I will pour out
in those days of my Spirit ; and they shall prophesy :
And I will show wonders in heaven above, and
signs in the earth beneath ; blood, and fire, and

vapour of smoke : The sun shall be turned into darkness, and the moon into blood, before that great and notable day of the Lord come : And it shall come to pass, that whosoever shall call on the name of the Lord shall be saved.

"Ye men of Israel, hear these words ; Jesus of Nazareth, a man approved of God among you by miracles and wonders and signs, which God did by him in the midst of you, as ye yourselves also know : Him, being delivered by the determinate counsel and foreknowledge of God, ye have taken, and by wicked hands have crucified and slain : Whom God hath raised up, having loosed the pains of death because it was not possible that he should be holden of it.

"For David speaketh concerning him, I foresaw the Lord always before my face, for he is on my right hand, that I should not be moved : Therefore did my heart rejoice, and my tongue was glad ; moreover also my flesh shall rest in hope : Because thou wilt not leave my soul in hell, neither wilt thou suffer thine Holy One to see corruption. Thou hast made known to me the ways of life ; thou shalt make me full of joy with thy countenance.

"Men and brethren, let me freely speak unto you

of the patriarch David, that he is both dead and buried, and his sepulchre is with us unto this day. Therefore being a prophet, and knowing that God had sworn with an oath to him, that of the fruit of his loins, according to the flesh, he would raise up Christ to sit on his throne ; He seeing this before spake of the resurrection of Christ, that his soul was not left in hell, neither his flesh did see corruption. This Jesus hath God raised up, whereof we all are witnesses." (Acts ii. 14-32.)

The sceptic never looks at the Resurrection through the eyes of the early disciples. Their complete and firm conviction was not the exclusive result of the testimony of human witnesses who did not understand that Christ would rise from the grave, and were bewildered to find the guard gone and the tomb empty ; but it was the work of the Holy Spirit. They had themselves been buried with Christ, and had risen with him—they had the witness within themselves. It is unjust to rob their testimony of its spiritual life, and base the evidence for their belief in the Resurrection upon the dead letter of their statements.

If the spiritual evidence, here indicated, be kept clearly in view, we may enter upon a consideration of the theories of the Resurrection with profit.

THE
TESTIMONY OF THE EVANGELISTS.

II

THE
TESTIMONY OF THE EVANGELISTS.

INTRODUCTION.

WE must be willing, if we would be true to ourselves, to believe all the facts, scientific, moral, and spiritual, that are or will be discovered. There are a multitude of known facts of which we are individually ignorant, and a greater multitude of which every living man is ignorant; but we must be constantly ready to accept every fact in God's universe, when it is discovered to us. The Duke of Argyll has truly said, "Indifference to truth in apparently the most distant spheres of thought may and does relax the most powerful springs of action."

Is the Resurrection of Jesus Christ from the dead an historical fact? If so, in spite of any prejudice we may have against a miracle, as such, we must accept it. If not, how can we account for the widespread belief that he did rise? What conditions must a document fulfil to be called "historical"? Or, better, what is history? How do we know that we read the Bible yesterday? How do we know there was a yesterday? How do we know anything of the past? Because God has given to us a faculty we call memory, "the miser of the brain." Perhaps we do not fully value this gift: it is as common as the air we breathe. Yet air and memory are equally vital to our existence. We often realise what a thing is worth when it is taken from us. The Rev. Robert Burton tells the story of a man who, although he had never been out of his native city of Milan, on being sentenced, by the Governor, not to stir beyond its gates, became so desperately miserable at a confinement he had fully enjoyed for sixty years that, obtaining no reprieve of the sentence, he died of grief. If the partial loss of liberty shackles life, the total loss of memory would reduce us to moving shadows, thrown from the hand of a deft conjuror upon the screen of time, illuminated only by the white disc of self-consciousness.

No memory; no miser to coffer up the precious

gold of our experience, no link with the moment now flying; no relations; father, mother, wife, child, forgotten ; no, not forgotten, never known. The past and the future a blank; the present a flash of consciousness. No yesterday; no history.

God has given to us memory. But we cannot rely solely upon memory for our knowledge of the past, for then our knowledge would be meagre and uncertain, even if every man possessed the memory of Samuel Johnson or Edward Gibbon.

Memory is the first faculty to fade at the touch of age. God has, therefore, enabled man to write, and the memory of the world is preserved on bricks, columns, slabs, medals, the leaves and barks of trees, and paper, and, within five hundred years, by printed books.

The faculties of memory and writing make history possible. But to produce a history of any movement, scene, or country, we must have witnesses, not only with these faculties, but able also accurately to observe and relate what they see. This means, of course, that they must have the opportunity of seeing or knowing what they describe. Other qualifications need not, for the purpose in view, detain us. And other conditions of history might be stated, but none of more importance than this. The witness should simply state what he saw, not what he wanted and expected to see ; nor should he confound what actually took place with any explanation of it.

The Reverend Father Didon has pointedly said : " In many cases, I prefer as a critic a simple peasant to a subtle and cautious man of learning. The first will tell me plainly what he has seen ; the other wants to give me an explanation. What interests the historian is first the fact, and afterwards, the explanation of the fact. In every hypothesis, before explaining phenomena, we need their verification ; and here I mistrust the over-cultivated man, who always looks to his own system. Such a man thinks himself in possession of a perfect instrument ; but he deceives himself : it is an admirable instrument for seeing what he wants, and for rejecting what does not suit him."[1]

It will be noticed that nothing has been said about " true " and " false " history. Now, history as defined would be " true history." " False history " is a contradiction of terms. It is true that much of what is called authentic history is

[1] Introduction to " Jesus Christ."

delusive. Inferences, impressions, prejudices, ignorance, opinions, mistakes are woefully mingled with
the facts. A man is good or bad, great or mean,
according to the taste of the historian. Henry VIII.
has two characters, according as the historian is a
rank Protestant or a Cardinal of the Roman
Church. Much "history" is confessedly imaginary.
Buried cities are rebuilt on paper, and dead movements are regalvanised into literary life. In such
cases the historian works from a basis of fact, but
his history is regarded as a literary "creation."
" The best historians," says Macaulay, " of later
years have been seduced from truth not by their
imagination, but by their reason."

With these reservations and drawbacks we have
happily nothing to do in these papers. The story
of the Resurrection lives in the memory of
Christendom ; it has so lived from the first Christian
Easter morning until now, and it has been preserved in writing, as Renan admits, from the age
immediately following the Resurrection itself. The
witnesses and the writings relating to the Resurrection conform to the strictest requirements, so
far as our immediate object is concerned. Our
immediate object is to read the events of the

Resurrection as they who are the best available witnesses, and, under the circumstances, the only possible witnesses, describe them. We are concerned with a single historical fact that is easily separated from any theory propounded to account for it. It is true that we shall find that the events have been stretched, clipped, and twisted to fit ingenious theories, but not by the witnesses themselves, nor by persons professing to believe in the fact itself. The witnesses to the Resurrection told what they actually saw with a simplicity and directness that are guarantees of their perfect sincerity and accuracy. It has been left to some sceptics to make these witnesses liars, insane visionaries, to distort and even invent facts, in order to avoid believing in the actual Resurrection of Jesus Christ.

THE TESTIMONIES COMBINED.

LET us read the testimony of the witnesses as related in the Gospels and Epistles, merely accepting these documents[1] because they contain the

[1]It is not necessary here, perhaps after the admissions of hostile critics it is not at all necessary, to discuss the age and authorship of these writings. For a very popular account of the results of modern criticism upon the authenticity of the Gospels see " The Gospel and its Witnesses," by Dr. Wace.

most authentic account of their testimony. Now
we must not misunderstand these witnesses. They
do not testify that they saw what no man could see,
the actual passage from death to life of Jesus
Christ. No one save Christ could speak about that
change; and no one could understand it, if told.
This does not weaken their testimony; on the
contrary, it strengthens it. They tell plainly all
they saw, without any transcendental inferences.

They saw Christ daily, spoke with Him, knew
Him, lived with Him, loved Him. No one can
make out a sound case of "mistaken identity."[1] They
could not be mistaken about Jesus of Nazareth,
"who went about doing good," and of whom His
enemies said, "Never man spake like this man."
This Jesus bled to death before their own eyes, and
before the eyes of ten thousand enemies. He was
buried to their certain knowledge, and three days
afterwards they saw Him alive, spoke with Him,
touched Him, ate and drank with Him, recognised
His voice, His familiar actions, His words of power
and authority. They knew Him again, as they
knew one another; they went forth at His command
to preach the Gospel of the Resurrection, and
sealed their testimony with their blood.

[1]See p.p. 78, 80 and 114.

Let us hear from their own lips what happened on the first Easter morning, merely that we may have the scenes before us as we investigate the theories started to account for their belief. Afterwards, we will listen to the non-Christian theorists.

We will join these early disciples and see the events *in the order of their occurrence* through their own eyes.[1]

We are, then, of the company of the women starting from Bethany, the hour before the dawn, bearing spices to anoint the body of our Master. The light of the beautiful stars pales before the faint flush of morning, as, choking with grief, we hurry along the dusty roads, the silence broken only by our footfalls and eager conversation. We anxiously ask each other, " Who shall roll away the

[1] Dr. Martineau (" Seat of Authority in Religion," pp. 358-377) adopts an entirely different method. He reads the events of Easter morning *in the order of the production of the Gospels and the Epistles* He says, " In order to approach this question to the best advantage, we must take up the documentary testimonies in the order of their production, and not in the historical order of appearances which they relate " (p. 366). Now, to approach the question in this way is, perhaps, to the "best advantage" of the theory he sets out to prove, but certainly not to the "best advantage" of the disciples and the actual facts of the Resurrection which they record. It is a distinctly unhistorical method. By this unhistorical method he is enabled to argue that—(1) the spiritual(?) appearance of Christ to Paul was *first* received,

stone?" for it was a very great stone which was rolled before the sepulchre and sealed. We walk quietly across the dewy grass in Joseph's garden, towards the stone tomb, and, looking up, see the stone rolled away from the sepulchre, and, entering in, find not the body of the Lord Jesus. The tomb is empty. What has happened? We, as yet, know not. We run with Mary Magdalene to find Peter and John, and say to them, "They have taken away the Lord out of the sepulchre, and we know not where they have laid Him." And we remain at the tomb with the other women, perplexed. Entering again into the sepulchre, we see two young men sitting on the right side, clothed in long white snowy garments. In fear, we bow down

and *afterwards* (2) the current belief in reincarnation clothed the spiritual appearance with bodily form, and that (3) a "persistent desire" for "palpable evidence" arising out of this belief in reincarnation, answered the question of the "why" of the empty grave, and of the disposal of the body, in harmony with its preconceived opinions. I have not seen this radically false method pointed out by any writer in answer to Dr. Martineau, but it seems to me to be the basis of his pet theory that the appearances were first of all spiritual, then "materialised" by the disciples. He everywhere contends, by subtle hints, that the material evidence for the Resurrection was a direct and conscious invention of the disciples. Now the order of the production of the Epistles and Gospels is *not* the order in which to see and study the events.

to the earth, and the men say, "Be not ye affrighted, for we know ye seek Jesus of Nazareth, which was crucified. Why seek ye the living with the dead? He is not here; He is risen, as He said. Remember how He spake unto you, when He was yet in Galilee, saying, 'The Son of Man must be delivered into the hands of sinful men, to be crucified, and the third day rise again.' Come, see the place where they laid Him, and go your way quickly, and tell His disciples and Peter that He is risen from the dead, and that He goeth before you into Galilee; there shall ye see Him, as He said unto you; lo! we have told you." We rush from the sepulchre in fearful joy, trembling and amazed, to tell the disciples. And Jesus meets us, saying, "All hail," and, falling down, we hold Him by the feet and worship Him. "Be not afraid," we hear His voice again: "go, tell my brethren that they go unto Galilee, and there shall they see Me." But when we tell the disciples, they receive our story as an idle tale. Now, Peter and John, running, come to the sepulchre. John first looks in, Peter enters boldly, then John goes in; they see the grave clothes, but the body is gone; then they return to their homes, wondering what has come to pass. Mary Magdalene stands outside weeping. Presently she stoops down and looks in, and two angels, one now sitting at the head and the other at the foot, say unto her, "Woman, why weepest thou?" She says, "Because they have taken away my Lord, and I know not where they have laid Him." Turning from the angels, she sees one whom she thinks is the gardener. "Woman," says he, "why weepest thou?" "Whom seekest thou?" "Sir, if thou hast borne Him hence, tell me where thou hast laid Him, and I will take Him away." Now He calls her by name, "Mary." "Master," she exclaims. It is Jesus, not the gardener. And as we hear Mary Magdalene tell the disciples, we see the look of incredulity in their faces, and they still "believed not." A few hours afterwards we are with two of the disciples, who are walking along the road towards Emmaus. A stranger joins us, and enters into the argument we are holding about Jesus of Nazareth. To our surprise, He does not appear to understand our conversation, and we explain to him the story of the trial and crucifixion, and the news brought by the women and disciples who had found the tomb empty, and Mary, who had seen a vision of angels. Then the stranger, beginning at Moses, shows us from all the prophets that these things were foretold concerning the Messiah. We listen with burning hearts until we reach Emmaus. Then we ask the stranger to stay with us, for He seems to want to go farther, and the day is far spent. And as we sit at meat, the stranger takes bread, and breaks it and blesses it, and gives it to us. It is Jesus Himself! and immediately we know Him, He vanishes out of sight.

We hurry back to Jerusalem, find the disciples assembled with shut doors, and tell them how we knew Him by the breaking of bread. And yet again they believe not.

Suddenly, but we are conscious of no movement, Jesus Himself is in the midst of us, and upbraids them with their unbelief and hardness of heart, " because they believed not them which had seen Him after He was risen." And we are terrified and affrighted, and suppose it is a spirit. And He saith unto us, " Why are ye troubled, and why do thoughts arise in your hearts? Behold my hands and my feet, that it is I myself; handle me and see, for a spirit hath not flesh and bones, as ye see Me have." Then he shows His hands, and His feet and side. "Have ye here any meat?" He asks, and we give Him a piece of a broiled fish and of a honeycomb, and He eats before us, and we yet believe not for joy and wonder. And He saith, "These are the words which I spake unto you, while I was yet with you, that all things must be fulfilled which were written in the law of Moses, and in the Prophets, and in the Psalms concerning me." "Thus it is written, and thus it behoved Christ to suffer, and to rise from the dead the third day, and that repentance and remission of sins should be preached in His name, among all nations, beginning at Jerusalem; and ye are witnesses of these things."

But Thomas, one of the twelve, was absent. The other disciples, therefore, said unto him, "We have seen the Lord." But he said unto them, "Except I shall see in his hands the print of the nails, and put my finger into the print of the nails, and thrust my hand into His side, I will not believe." After eight days Jesus appeared again to the disciples in like manner, Thomas being present. Then saith He to Thomas, "Reach hither thy finger and behold my hands, and reach hither thy hand and thrust it into my side, and be not faithless, but believing." And Thomas exclaims, " My Lord and My God." "Thomas," says Jesus, "because thou hast seen me, thou hast believed; blessed are they that have not seen, and yet have believed."

We now join the company of Simon Peter, and Thomas called Didymus, and Nathaniel of Cana in Galilee, and the sons of Zebedee, and two others of the disciples at the sea of Tiberias. Peter saith, " I go a-fishing," and all reply, "We go with thee." We spend the night on the sea, but not a fish is caught. In the morning Jesus stands on the shore, but we know not that it is Jesus. Then He asks us, " Children, have ye any meat ? " We answer, " No." Then he saith to us, " Cast the net on the right side of the ship and ye shall find." And we cast, and are not able to draw it for the multitude of fishes. Therefore, John exclaims to Peter, " It is the Lord." Peter, who is naked, folds his fisher's coat about him, and casts himself into the sea. But we go in the ship, dragging the net with fishes. Jesus saith unto us, " Bring of the fishes which ye have now caught," for there was a fire of coals on the shore, and fish laid thereon, and bread.

Peter draws the net to land, full of great fishes, a
hundred and fifty and three. Jesus says to us,
"Come and dine," and none of us dared ask him,
"Who art thou?" knowing it is the Lord. And
Jesus comes, takes the bread and fish, and gives
it to us. This is the third appearance to the
disciples.

And now we go with the eleven into a mountain,
where Jesus has appointed to meet them. And
there above five hundred brethren see Him at once,
and when they see Him they worship Him, but
some doubt.

"After that, Jesus was seen of James, then of all
the apostles, to whom also He showed Himself
alive, after His passion, by many infallible proofs,
being seen of them forty days, and speaking of the
things pertaining to the Kingdom of God."

Such is the story of the Evangelists. In the
words of Lessing, "In these records is fixed for
ever the startled joy of the Church at the great
news of the Resurrection. Here, as in a festal
choir, though the voices seem at times to be
confused, isolated, or contrary, yet they are all
pursuing one theme in full, grand, and blissful
harmony. We may clearly see the rich unity of
the one Resurrection history amid all its details."

THE SWOON THEORY.

(*From the Late Cardinal Manning, to the Author, October 29th, 1891.*)

As to the 'swoon theory' it is to me more incredible than nine resurrections.

That a man should swoon in and after crucifixion piercing in the side, and draining of blood in the midst of 10,000 eyes is in itself a miracle, surpassing all experience, involving a suspension of all senses, in broad daylight, a of both friends and enemies.

It is to me a stupendous fable.

III

THE SWOON THEORY.

We may take every advantage of the fact that sceptics have felt the necessity of propounding some theory[1] to account for our belief in the Resurrection of Jesus Christ. *Something* happened as the dawn broke upon the dark hills of Moab and stole into the beautiful garden of Joseph of Arimathæa on the first Lord's Day, something that transformed the disciples, and through them the world. The disciples believed that " the angel ot

[1] "The greatest critic of our century has acknowledged that for the disciples Jesus' resurrection had become a firm and incontestable certainty, but the same critic has had to renounce any hope of explaining the phenomenon. Historical enquiry, however, cannot rest content with this. The history of Christendom cannot begin with an insoluble enigma. At the close of our narrative we again find ourselves face to face with a dilemma; either indisputable facts must be left unexplained, or else historical inquirers, who care nothing for this philosophic dogma, which declares miracles to be impossible, must be permitted to attempt their explanation, even when that cannot be done without the assumption of a unique divine miracle."— Weiss, L. of C., Vol. 3., P. 383.

the Lord descended from heaven, and came and
rolled back the stone from the door " of the Holy
Sepulchre, and that Christ arose from the dead.
This was their "theory" of the Resurrection ; and
it is our " theory." " The rise of that belief in the
disciples is," writes Dr. Strauss, "at all events
perfectly explained if we regard the Resurrection
of Jesus as an outward miraculous occurrence such
as the Evangelists describe it . . . . . adopt
this view (that Christ did actually rise) as our own,
however, we cannot."[1] *Something* happened on
the first Easter Day—it was the Resurrection of
our Blessed Master. " The man who believes this
can go forward through life; he is armed for
defence; he may grow great, and nothing can stay
him. The disciple of Jesus has become the
sovereign of the world." *Didon.*

The Resurrection of Jesus Christ may be denied
(*a*) by denying the reality of His death, (*b*) by
admitting the reality of His death, but by denying
the physical reality of His appearance, (*c*) by
regarding the story of the Resurrection as a fabri-
cation.

[1]Life of Jesus.

The Resurrection did not take place if Jesus Christ did not die upon the cross. The advocates of the Swoon Theory say that he did not die.

Something more than an historical interest attaches to this theory. It is perhaps the first explanation which may arise in the mind of one who rejects as insufficient the testimony for the actual Resurrection of Jesus Christ.[1] Incredible as it may seem to those who are acquainted with the history of the hypothesis of " the apparent death " of Jesus Christ, it is actively propagated in sermons and leaflets[2] amongst the cultured Theists who to this day listen Sunday by Sunday to their courageous and genial pastor, the Rev. Charles Voysey. Why should the " Swoon Theory," turned out of doors by recent critics in Germany, where it was ingeniously defended in the first

---

[1] " It is not an unnatural explanation ; it is ever apt to rise before our minds when we doubt a real Resurrection, and it is therefore necessary to speak of it."—Prof. Milligan, " The Resurrection of our Lord," p. 80.

[2] Since the publication of a part of this chapter in " The King's Own" we have received a leaflet from the Rev. C. Voysey, containing an outline of "The Swoon Theory," which he offers for " free distribution " at the request of his congregation.

half of this century, be given shelter and defended by a cultured English Clergyman ? Difficult as this question is to answer, there is another question still more difficult. How can a body of intelligent people, such as worship in the Theistic Church, Piccadilly, not only patiently listen to a defence of this hypothesis, but enthusiastically applaud its defence ? May the answer be found in the fact that this defender of an exploded hypothesis explains it without one word about its origin ! ! Indeed, he leaves his hearers and readers to suppose that he is its author, and his admirers seem to be unaware of evidence to the contrary.

It may then be profitable to recall the fact that its chief advocate in Germany was Dr. Heinrich E. G. Paulus,[1] (1828), and among less prominent supporters were Venturini, Bahrdt, and to some extent Schleiermacher. Strauss, in his "New Life of Jesus"[2] now rejects it with scornful laughter. In England no great critic has ever adopted it, but the author of " Supernatural Religion " says, " whilst we do not ourselves adopt this explanation, it must be clearly repeated that, were the only

[1]"Das Leben Jesu." (pub. at Heidelberg), p. 277, and his "Exegetisches Handbuch," p. 929.
[2]4th Ed., p. 735

alternative to do so, or to fall back upon the hypothesis of a miracle, we should ¦consider it preferable.[1]

Now, according to the theory popularised by Dr. Paulus, the shepherds, who were abiding in the field keeping watch over their flock by night when Mary brought forth her first-born Son the Saviour of the world, did *not* see or hear a multitude of the heavenly host; the plains of Bethlehem were *not* flooded with golden light, for the glory of the Lord did *not* shine round about them—it was simply an *ignis fatuus*, or a meteor. The miracle at the marriage in Cana of Galilee was a joke; the company could not see the difference between water and wine in the twilight. Lazarus, and the daughter of Jairus a ruler of the synagogue, and the dead youth who was carried out to the gate of the city of Nain, were not really dead—they were in a trance or a swoon. Jesus Christ did *not* die upon the Cross, He only fainted; it was a death-like torpor from which he ultimately

[1]Complete Ed., Vol. 3, p. 524.

recovered under the influence of the myrrh and aloes in the cool rock-hewn vault. This is the natural theory of interpretation—it is the critical separation of what Paulus calls *fact* from what he calls *opinion*. "The great difficulty, for a man," says Didon, "is that he should submit himself to the Gospel; and his greatest temptation, to desire to transform it as he pleases according to his own systems."

Jesus did not die upon the cross ! ! Let us look at the arguments in favour of this monstrous assumption. If He did not die upon the cross, did He deceive the soldiers who crucified Him, His enemies, and His friends? Bahrdt did not hesitate to make Him a deceiver; but Dr. Paulus was too much impressed by His beautiful character to adopt that base opinion. Yet Bahrdt was logical. If the belief in the Resurrection of Jesus was based upon His temporary recovery from a faint, He not only did nothing to disabuse His disciples,[1] who had left all to follow Him, but He

---

[1] "The responsibility of the deception upon which tidings of the resurrection was founded, is taken from the disciples but brought into suspicious proximity with the person of Jesus."—Weiss, "Life of Christ," Vol. 3, p. 384.

"The apostles were either miserable victims of deceit, or with Jesus, themselves deceivers."—Keim, J. of N., Vol.6. p. 330

distinctly persuaded them,[1] under the most pathetic circumstances, to believe what He must have known was a desperate lie, unless the voice of consciousness is a liar. And we can scarcely doubt that some of the disciples were not only not deceived, but must have promoted the deception.

Every item that lends, even in appearance only, the shadow of support to the Swoon Theory has been seized upon by its advocates.

In the inhuman punishment by crucifixion, the victim generally lived through the agony and shame for four or five days. History has been ransacked to find illustrations of this fact. The fabulous story of Sister Francisca who was crucified a score of times, and the merciful effort of Josephus[2] who succeeded in saving, with the utmost medical care, only one prisoner out of three, who were crucified, who had been hanging but a few hours upon their crosses, are of equal

[1] John, xx, 27, Luke xxiv, 25, 27, 46.

[2] " When I was sent by Titus Cæsar with Cerealius, and a thousand horsemen, to a certain village, called Thecoa, in order to know whether it were a place fit for a camp, as I came back, I saw many natives crucified ; and remembered three of them, as my former acquaintances. I was very sorry at this in my mind, and went with tears in my eyes to Titus and told him of them; so he immediately commanded them to be taken down, and to have the greatest care taken of them in order to their recovery. Yet two of them died under the physicians hands, while the third recovered."—The Life of Josephus by Himself Whiston's Ed. 1737. ¶ 75.

value for the critic,[1] who sits in judgment upon the witnesses for the Resurrection of Jesus. Jesus only remained upon the cross a few hours. In His youthful body "weakened by no passions, the abode of a cheerful pious mind, the vital forces, though suddenly strained by excessive irritation and maltreatment, were not exhausted. He became torpid, respiration and consciousness were suspended; but He could not have been dead."[2] But there were special circumstances which shortened[3] Jesus' life. For example, his agony in the garden of Gethsemane, when the sweat fell from Him like drops of blood upon the ground. He was arrested at midnight, and by brutal men was blindfolded and struck in the hall of the High Priest's palace—treatment not meted out to Barabbas; then

[1]Paulus.

[2]Keim paraphrasing Paulus, J. of N., Vol. 6, p. 327.

[3]Various immediate causes of the early death of Jesus have been suggested : Renan says "The delicate organization of Jesus preserved Him from the slow agony of crucifixion, every thing tends to show that the instantaneous rupture of a vessel in the heart killed Him, at the end of three hours . . . . His head fell upon His breast and he expired."—"Life of Jesus." p. 183.

See also Dr. Stroud " Physical causes of the death of Christ" The late Sir Andrew Clarke valued this book, but Bishop Westcott ("Gospel of St. John," p. 279) regards the arguments of Dr. Stroud upon the blood and water which came from our Saviour's side, as inadequate and inconsistent with the real facts.

the prolonged and exciting nature of His trial; His
wearying journeys from the High Priest to Pilate,
from Pilate to Herod, and back to Pilate—and
His want of sleep and perhaps of food ; the horse-
play of some of the soldiers of Herod; and His
inhuman treatment by the whole band of soldiers
under Pilate, who stripped Him, pressed a wreath
of thorns upon His head, spat in His face, and
struck Him with a reed. The effect of the
scourging, awful in every case, was terrible upon
the delicate body of Jesus. He could not, like
other malefactors, carry His cross to Calvary.
And He was conscious to the last moment of the
whole agony of crucifixion, He refused to drink
the wine mingled with myrrh, but drank the
bitter cup which His Father gave Him.

What can we say about the Lord's inner and
mysterious sufferings ? We believe that He was
crushed to death by the weight of our sins, which
He voluntarily bore in love. With Isaiah we say,
" He bore our griefs, and carried our sorrows; He
was wounded for our transgressions, and bruised
for our iniquities; the chastisement of our peace
was laid upon him; and by His stripes we are
healed." It was our Saviour's declared intention

to die,[1] in order to redeem us from the curse of the law and to vanquish death.[2]   The unbeliever who overlooks this cardinal point, and says that Jesus did not die, does not understand Christian teaching.

In his lust of negation he would empty the loving sacrifice of our Lord of every atom of its thrice blessed meaning, and make Him in the dread hour of death, when even a criminal is honest, act in violent contradiction to every word and action of His life, a sickening spectacle that would shake our faith in God and man. Jesus, he says, after praying to His Father to forgive the soldiers who drove the nails through His hands and feet, "only pretended to die."[3]

Of course, doubt is thrown upon those parts of the gospel narrative which disagree with this wild assumption, or they are used in a sense which does violence to their context.   He was spared the breaking of the legs—a point, reads the critical

[1] John x, 15, Luke xviii, 33, and elsewhere.   Bishop Ellicott says "Crucifixion itself would not necessarily cause death for several days, nor indeed at all ; but Jesus had by His own will committed His Spirit to His Father."

[2] "First Christ died for our sins ; secondly He hath been raised and He lives for ever, These truths may not be separated from each other.   God hath joined them together ; no man may put them asunder." Milligan, "The Resurrection of the dead," p. 10.

[3] Bahrdt.

Paulus, in His favour. " The leg-breaking," says the author of " Supernatural Religion," " disappears with the lance-thrust."[1] " It is mentioned in the fourth Gospel," he continues, for " dogmatic reasons."[2] Then, supposing the soldiers did pierce his side, the wound[3] may not have been dangerous. The wounds of the nails, of course, had the well-known beneficial result of blood letting ; and supposing that His feet were not pierced there can be no difficulty in believing that He put on the gardener's clothes, met Mary in the Garden on the first Easter morning, walked three-score furlongs to Emmaus in the afternoon, and in the evening returned to Jerusalem and met His disciples in the upper room ! He perhaps would be a little weak when He recovered from His swoon, but supposing that His friends Joseph and Nicodemus rendered Him a little medical assistance in the Sepulchre ! and if these Essene friends were clad in "white

[1] Vol. 3, p. 523.

[2] It is the constant and vicious assumption of hostile critics that the gospel writers deliberately invent sayings and scenes to suit some set purpose. Do the critics in this unconsicously reveal their own methods ?

[3] It is generally admitted that the lance used (probably the long lance of a horseman) would have caused a deep wound. This is certain from the fact that our Lord invited Thomas to thrust his hand into His side. John xx, 27.

robes" it is conceivable that the women who loved Him may have supposed them to be "angels!" Then it must be remembered that the tomb was a new one, that He was wrapped in strong spices which would "revive"[1] Him, that clear Jerusalem air played freely about the tomb! and that the earthquake, which probably did not happen, would certainly have helped to arouse Him and roll away the stone from the mouth of the tomb.

Interment, as we know, does not exclude the possibility of a lethargy; perhaps under such happy and healthy circumstances, not even that of recovery! It requires no great stretch of faith to suppose that when He visited His disciples, as He probably did occasionally, they supposed He had "risen from the dead" And then supposing He discovered, for He had an "acute mind," that His death "had set the crown upon His work," He would, no doubt, have soon withdrawn "into inpenetrable obscurity," perhaps to save His disciples the sight of His weakness and to die unseen. Of course, He returned from His hiding

[1]The point has been disputed, the spices may have had a "stupefying and suffocating" effect.

place about a year later to "appear" to Paul and then " He was heard of no more." Then supposing the disciples found ready ears for their story, which they themselves truly believed, the ground is cleared for the foundation of the Christian Church, and the Gospel of the Resurrection ! !

Then SUPPOSE——but enough.

Origen speaks about a supposition of an "apparent death,"[1] for it is true of this " modern objection " to Christianity, as of a thousand others, that it is as old as unbelief, and was conceived in sin. " In addition," he wrote in reply to Celsus, " to other causes for the crucifixion of Jesus, this also may have contributed to His dying a conspicuous death upon the cross, that no one might have it in his power to say that He voluntarily withdrew from the sight of men, and seemed only die, without really doing so; but, appearing again, made a jugglers trick of the Resurrection from the dead."[2]

But it is encouraging and instructive to weigh the reasons which the great modern critics, who have some other theory to support, balance against this one. The author of " Supernatural Religion,"

[1]But it was not seriously believed.
[2]"Origen Contra Celsum," Anti-Nicene Library, Vol. xxiii,p.60

who confesses that he would rather believe the
swoon theory than the reality of the resurrection,
admits that the serious objection that it is not
natural to suppose, after such intense and
protracted fatigue and anxiety, followed by the
most cruel agony on the cross, agony both of soul
and body, Jesus could have appeared to his
disciples and have conveyed to them the impression
that He had conquered death, is "partly true."
But a more "powerful objection" presents itself
to his mind. "We cannot easily persuade ourselves," he writes, "that such a teacher could
have renounced his work and left no subsequent
trace of His existence."[1] Strauss feels that this
objection which is only "partly true" possesses
"great weight."

"A person who had crept half-dead from the
tomb, crawled about ill, wanting medical assistance, bandages, strengthening and indulgence, and
who at last, nevertheless, succumbed to His
sufferings, could not possibly make upon the
disciples the impression of a conqueror over death
and the grave, the Prince of Life, which lay at the

[1]Vol. 3, p. 525.

foundation of their subsequent ministry; a resuscitation of such a kind would only have tended to weaken the impression which, in life and death, He had made upon them, and, at most, could only have given it an elegiac voice, but could, by no possibility have changed their mourning into enthusiasm, or elevated their reverence into worship."[1]

Keim, who thinks that the strongest point in favour of the theory is the absence of formal proof of death, finds such impossibilities in the theory that he impatiently exclaims " Then there is the most impossible thin of all; the poor, weak, sick Jesus, with diffi. .y holding Himself erect, in hiding, disguised, and finally dying—this Jesus, an object of faith, of exalted emotion, of the triumph of his adherents, a risen conqueror and Son of God ! Here, in fact the theory begins to grow paltry, absurd, worthy only of rejection."[2]

Among Christians the theory has, no doubt, appeared as an insult to common sense; and it has received scant treatment, mainly because unbelievers have themselves blown it out of the

[1]Life of Jesus, p. 225, 1894 Ed.
[2]Keim, J. of N., Vol. 3, p. 330.

water. "At the present day it is not worth while," says Weiss " to dissolve this phantasy destitute of all historical meaning, in the destruction of which Strauss earned his laurels as a critic."

And Prof. Geo. G. Stokes, writing to the Author, says:—

" When I closed my letter I had not thought of what you said about the Swoon Theory. Of all the attempted explanations of the admitted facts, I think there is none which to my mind seems so opposed to common sense as that.

" With respect to the condition of Jesus of Nazareth after the Crucifixion, we may suppose— That He died, and there was an end of Him; or that He was not killed, but only swooned, and afterwards recovered, and resumed His natural life; or that He was raised from the dead in a supernatural manner, to a kind of life which, being supernatural in its commencement, would seem to be very likely supernatural in its conditions.

" It is not, I believe, disputed that His apostles and other disciples, rightly or wrongly, believed that in spite of His crucifixion, and, at least, apparent death, He afterwards lived.

" It is not, I believe, disputed, that rather than disown this belief they submitted to persecutions, and death itself in various forms.

" Consider what motives could be conceived to induce men to incur all this suffering.

" On the first supposition we must suppose that somehow or other they came to believe that Jesus rose from the dead. We cannot imagine them to have submitted to persecution and death merely to support a lie, which they knew to be a lie, from from which they could gain nothing at all.

" But if they believed so strongly that He rose—though He did nothing of the kind—what can we imagine to have produced such a belief? According to the accounts we have (and they are the only accounts) they were altogether disconcerted by the Crucifixion. All their expectations seemed to be dashed to the ground. ' We thought that it should have been He that should have redeemed Israel.' How are we to account for the sudden change from abject despondency to joyful assurance of a thing which never happened, and which, false though it were, so engaged their affections that

they were ready to, and did actually, die for it ?
Difficult as this may be to account for, the second
supposition seems to me to involve far greater
difficulties.　First, there is the inherent difficulty
of the supposition itself.　The centurion, the
soldiers, all about Him, many of whom must have
been used to such scenes, without any exception
that we know of, thought that He was dead. Were
not those on the spot better judges than 19th
century theorisers ?　Then, again, what of the
spear wound in the side—a wound which must
have been a very severe one, as it stated that
blood and water came out of it, whatever the
medical explanation and import of that may have
been, about which I do not venture to express my
opinion, as I am not a medical man or physiologist?

" The faint, if faint it were, must have lasted a
very long time. I am aware that in cases of
catalepsy a person may remain for a long time
apparently dead, and afterwards come to. Now,
as I said, I am no medical man, but I do not
recollect ever to have read in the newspaper, or
elsewhere, or to have heard of a cataleptic state
having been brought about by violence. Pain
may cause a person to faint; but in such cases I

imagine that the person before long either dies of syncope or comes to. Great loss of blood may cause unconsciousness for a time, but on resuming consciousness the person would be weak, not able for such activity as would in any way fit the narrative.

" But the formidable inherent difficulty of the supposition is only the prelude to difficulties perhaps even greater still.

" Waiving this difficulty, let us suppose that Jesus merely swooned, and after an unusually long time came to. On this supposition the Resurrection was a purely natural process; the life He came back to was the ordinary natural human life, subject to the same conditions as the ordinary life of men in general. But this does not square with the narrative. He is represented as coming and going in some mysterious manner, utterly unlike the ordinary intercourse of one man with his fellow men. What possible motives could the writers have had for so misrepresenting the intercourse of the Teacher with His disciples? And if they knew that His re-appearance was nothing more than a natural revival from a faint, what possible motive could they have had for asserting what they knew to be be a lie, that He had risen from the dead ? They had only to tell the truth and their persecutors would not have cared about it, as it would prove nothing, and they themselves might have escaped scot free.

" To my mind, the supposition of revival from a faint, so far from assisting in getting rid of the supernatural, enormously increases the difficulty of so doing.

" There remains the third alternative. On this supposition the whole thing hangs together, and is self-consistent. Of course, it involves the non-rejection of the supernatural as such. But the historical evidence of the Resurrection is not to be separated from the body of Christian doctrine of which it forms a part. The two are to be regarded as complimentary portions of a complete whole. And the comprehension of this whole involves the exercise not of the intellectual powers alone, but also of the moral faculties. Without the union of the two, the positive evidence of the Resurrection is, in my opinion, incomplete."[1]

Did Jesus Christ die upon the cross? No one living at the time doubted the reality of His death

[1] This Letter is strictly Copyright.

after Pilate had given the body to Joseph for burial. It is not suggested that a single person of the great company which followed Him to Calvary, nor that one of the rulers who derided Him and called on Him to save Himself as He hung upon the cross, nor that the soldiers who did not break His legs "because He was dead already," nor that the keepers who watched the sealed sepulchre, nor that the women who started for the tomb very early in the morning of the first day of the week bearing spices to embalm the body of their Master, nor that one of "the twelve"-not excepting Thomas,-nor that Judas, had he not hanged himself immediately after the condemnation, nor that a single sincere critic before the rise of modern Rationalism had or could have had a serious doubt as to the reality of the death of Jesus Christ. Why then should it be doubted after eighteen hundred years?

THE VISION AND APPARITION THEORIES.

"It can hardly be expected that the common sense of the public will permanently accept any of the present critical explanations of the alleged appearance of Christ after death. It will not accept the view of Strauss, according to which the mythopœic faculty creates a legend without an author and without a beginning ; so that when St. Paul says He was seen of Cephas, then of "the twelve," he is repeating about acquaintances of his own an extraordinary assertion which was never originated by any definite person on any definite grounds, but which somehow proved so persuasive to the very men who were best able to contradict it that they were willing to suffer death for its truth. Nor will the world be contented with the theory according to which Christ was never killed at all, but was smuggled by some unknown disciples into the room where the twelve sat at meat, and then disappeared unaccountably from the historic scene, after crowning a divine life with a sham resurrection. Nor will men continue to believe that the faithful were again and again convinced that their master was standing visibly among them, but thought this because there was an accidental noise, or a puff of air, or even an atmospheric effect. One wishes that the robust Paley, with his twelve men of known probity were alive to deal with hypotheses like these. The Apostles were not so much like a British jury as Paley imagined them. But they were more like a British jury than like a parcel of hysterical monomaniacs."

F. W. H. Myers on "Renan and Miracles." Nineteenth Century, vol. x.

IV

THE VISION AND APPARITION THEORIES.

THE VISION THEORY.

Dr. Martineau makes a considerable effort to show that Jesus, in the estimation of the disciples, could not die. The impression he made upon their minds and hearts was so overwhelming that death could not remove it. Even after they saw him die, they "instinctively believed" him to be living, not of course in this world "but in another."

"Every other human life has finished with the earth at death," says Keim, but "tradition makes a difference in the case of Jesus."[1]

The Author of "Supernatural Religion," whose pages are lacking in the glow of charity as well as

[1] J. of N. vol. vi, p. 274.

of faith, recognises " the fact that, although its nature and extent are very indefinite, there existed an undoubted belief that, after his death, Jesus was seen alive."

" The story of a great man ends at His grave. He enters by death into an invisible world which is closed against us. We see Him no more, we hear Him no more. But," continues the devout Didon, "just as the birth of Jesus bears no resemblance to ours, so neither does His death resemble our death."[1]

" It was not possible," says the Apostle Paul, " that he should be holden of death." The point is undisputed. Believer and unbeliever admit that Christ lived after death. The believer that He actually arose from the dead to a real life on earth, the unbeliever that He lived and still lives by His personal influence, His works and teachings, in the minds of His disciples. The supernatural element is not necessarily absent from either view.

His triumph over death is surely strengthened by the discovery of the empty tomb. The fact,

[1] Jesus Christ, vol. ii. p. 364.

never doubted by the disciples and regarded by the best critics as beyond reasonable doubt, is that within forty hours of the burial of Jesus, the tomb in which He was buried was found empty. "This is altogether independent of the questions whether the grave had been emptied by resurrection or by an accident, whether the one who appeared was the risen or the actual Jesus, or perhaps only an ocular illusion consequent upon the report of the women; it is simply the discovery of the empty grave which is here discussed, and this appears so probable that many critics, not only of the Right but even of the Left, are able to regard it as certain or incontrovertible."[1]

Keim and other critics hold strongly to the position that the belief in the resurrection arose out of the fact of the empty grave. A Christian writer also oratorically argues that the Christian Church is figuratively built over the empty tomb, I suppose as the Church of the Holy Sepulchre at Jerusalem, at the present hour, covers, it is alleged, the actual tomb. Now, whilst the importance of the emptiness of the tomb must not

[1]Keim, vol. vi. p. 297.

be weakened,it is surely contrary to the chronology of the facts to believe that the disciples said within themselves—'the grave is empty, therefore Christ has risen.' They were startled and bewildered to find the stone rolled away and the body gone. But it was only after they had seen the living Jesus,[1] that they slowly understood the meaning of the empty tomb. *It was the sight of their master alive not of His empty tomb which formed the starting point of their faith.* They do not even appear to have troubled about preserving the grave where He had once lain in the sleep of death, as we do with our great dead. They left the tomb as their master left it—behind Him, and began to live a new life.

We must be cautious,however, in estimating the influence of the different events of the resurrection upon the disciples.

Dr. Martineau must credit the disciples with his own subtle philosophical mind if He imagines that they built up their belief upon the plan which

---

[1]"When He was risen from the dead, His disciples believed the Scriptures. For as yet they knew not the Scripture, that He must rise again from the dead." (Comp John ii. 22, xx. 9).

he draws with some show of architectural beauty.
He holds that the first faith of the disciples was
independent of any material evidence. He argues,
like Keim, that Jesus could not die in the minds of
the disciples. He was always living to them, and
they invented, more or less consciously, the
external material evidence to support their inward
and spiritual belief. "The hovering of interest
about the tomb is the incipient materializing of
the first faith."[1] This is the starting point of
his visionary theories. Here the Gospels
clash with these hypotheses. Faith in the
Resurrection did not start in the minds of the
Apostles independent of material evidence. The
living Jesus whose face they knew, whose voice
they heard, whose feet they held, who walked with
them, whom they saw with their own eyes, whose
wounds were open to their touch, who ate and
drank before them, was surely material evidence,
and material evidence of which their faith was not
independent, material evidence which gave rise to
their faith. *There is not a particle of evidence to
show that they believed He was risen before they
saw Him alive.* The chronology of the facts, and

[1] Seat of Authority in Religion, p. 370.

the facts themselves forbid such an assumption. And the state of mind of the disciples, well illustrated in the case of the two disciples, Cleopas and perhaps his wife, who were walking to Emmaus when Jesus met them, makes, it has been long admitted, the supposition psychologically impossible.

Here, in passing, it may be as well to note that Martineau and other critics wish to show that in Paul's estimation there was no difference between the appearance of Jesus Christ to him and the Christophanies to the first disciples. "It is the task of history" writes Keim, "to give the facts (of the appearances) as they are received from the hand of Paul; to accept from the more doubtful sources, the Gospels, whatever is in harmony with Paul, to exclude and to place by itself as glorifying mythical history, whatever is contradicted by his presentations."[1] Not so would Paul have treated the

[1] J of N., vol. 6, p. 280.

appearances to his fellow disciples. Nor is such treatment the task of history. Paul says, He (Christ) appeared to Cephas ; then to the twelve, then he appeared to above five hundred brethren at once of whom the greater part remain until now, but some are fallen asleep ; then he appeared to James; then to all the Apostles ; and last of all, as unto one born out of due time, he appeared to me also.[1]

" This inclusion of all under the same category could hardly be, if the writer were conscious that his own experience, as inward and spiritual, was strongly contrasted with that of others as a return of the earthly body from the grave, etc. . . if the same word " vision " is to mean the same thing, the " appearance" to Peter and James and the twelve was no other than the " appearances "

---

[1] I Cor. xv. 3, 8. Keim thinks that "it is above all evident that Paul supplies the complete list and definite sequence of the appearances (p. 292). But this is contradicted by the whole circumstances" under which Paul wrote to the Corinthian Christians, and the whole tone of his letter. Prof. Milligan puts the citation of these witnesses in its true position when he says :—"The Corinthian Christians must depend upon positive assertion *confirmed by undeniable experience of the result*, (italics ours) even the witnesses of the Resurrection of Christ are cited less as witnesses to prove a point, than as witnesses who tell an old story."

to Paul."[1]   Keim puts the same point in another
way. " There is a marked distinction," he says
" between Paul and them. Paul[2] in mentioning
the   resurrection   appearances   of   Jesus,   has
determinedly excluded the speaking of Jesus, the
sitting   and   walking   together,   the   eating   and
handling, every gross representation of a restora-
tion of the previous corporeity of Jesus .   .   .
there is no doubt that he conceived the coming of
Jesus   to   them   as   exactly   similar   to   Jesus
appearances to him."   But he is inclined to admit
that the Gospels " undoubtedly assume "   " a

[1]Martineau, p. 368.

[2]Keim with every other sober critic admits that the first
Epistle of Paul to the Corinthians takes us back to a date
"which was separated by only four years from the great
events of the death and resurrection of Jesus." He adds that
"it will not be said that it was to Paul's interest to prove the
resurrection; and that his interest, his credulity, his prejudice
which his belief in his own vision of Christ had already
excited in favour of the appearances of Christ to others—
made him willing, nay passionately anxious to register all
and every saying and myth, whilst he was fain to pass by
opposed voices and facts. Such a suspicion is forbidden by
his whole character, by his acute understanding, which was
entirely free from fanaticism, by the form of his careful,
cautious, measured, plain representation, by the simple
unassuming details of his statements ; and above all, by the
favourable general impression his report produces, and by
the powerful corroboration which accompanied it in the clear
consistent, universal belief of early Christendom, and
particularly in the testimony of a host of living eye witnesses,"
J. of N. vol. vi., p. 280.

reality, in fact a certain corporeity, of the appearances,"[1]

Now, it is quite clear to an unprejudiced reader of the Gospel and of Paul's account of his seeing Jesus, that it was very natural for the disciples of Jesus who knew Him and lived with Him in the flesh, who were daily accustomed to hear His voice and witness His actions, to observe and speak of his sitting and walking, and eating and speaking, and of His invitation to handle him and see that He was not merely an immaterial spirit; whilst Paul would see Him as a *person*— as the Risen Christ descended from Heaven—not necessarily less corporeal but more Heavenly. The disciples would see Him as a brother whose every familiar look and gesture was dear to them ; and they would love, as the Emmaus disciples, to tell how they knew Him in the breaking of bread. Paul, with justifiable emphasis, asked "Have I not seen the Lord?" But he did not, by this emphasis, "determinedly exclude" the peculiar and familiar

[1] J. of N., vol. 6, p. 290.

associations of the Lord's appearances[1] to His more immediate disciples. His words even seem to imply that he recognised the different circumstances and the different way in which Christ appeared to the other disciples. Nevertheless he had *seen* the Lord ; the appearance to him was of as much importance as the appearance to the elder disciples. He had not seen Him on the third day when He came out of the tomb; he had not seen Him as one who had just then returned to a life on earth ; he had not demanded to see the print of the nails and the spear wound; but he had *seen* Him, of that fact there was no doubt in his mind, neither in the minds of the other disciples. It is only the critic who, on some philosophical ground has arrived at the conclusion

[1] " His manifestations on the earth and His appearing from Heaven must have been distinguished from one another by a necessity of nature," (Steinmeyer, p. 322) Strauss evades this distinction entirely. He says " the appearances, which the elder disciples had had soon after the resurrection of Jesus, were of the same nature as that which had been, though at a later time, participated in by himself." (Life of Jesus, page 226). Keim admits that " Paul himself places an interval between this appearance (to him) and the previous ones (to the elder disciples.)" J. of N., p. 288.

that a miracle cannot happen, who makes the disciples see only what Paul saw, and makes Paul's sight an inner vision without any external reality. It is the upholder of the vision theory who " determinedly excludes" the visible, tangible realities from the Gospel Christophanies. The limits of the first strange sight of Paul were not the limits of the long and loving sight of His first chosen disciples. They followed their Master when Paul was Saul the persecutor. They saw when Paul was blind, and he was blinded that he might see. Paul's first sight was of Christ glorified; the elder disciples saw Him in His humility as the carpenter's son, and when they saw Him as the Risen Saviour, they still recognised the Son of Mary, and His body that cruel hands maltreated. When *they* saw Jesus they would recall the way they had travelled with Him from His home in Nazareth to the Cross at the end of the Sorrowful Way. It was no vision destitute of reality. It was no inward vision to Paul. They all saw Christ and the sight in the one case revived an almost dead faith, and in the other case transformed the persecutor into a magnificent defender of the faith, the " merciless fanatic," as Holsten calls him, "into a patient sufferer full of world-subduing, self-consuming love."[1] If the disciples in the Upper Room at Jerusalem on the evening of the first Easter day had seen what Paul saw, they would have recognised their Master. If Paul had been Thomas he would have exclaimed "My Lord and My God."

Peter's sight of the empty tomb, confirms the Paul's sight of the ascended Christ. "Paul, says Keim, "is in the main silent as to the proceedings in and at the grave." It may be so, but the argument of silence is vicious, and often leads to the mutual destruction of witnesses. We have seen why Paul does not detail all the circumstances surrounding the Resurrection. In this case the silence is golden. It is in complete harmony with his purpose and his position. But it is worthy of note that this method of judging Peter by Paul[2]

[1] "Baur at the close of his life-work, and to the annoyance of many, expressed the opinion that no analysis, either psychological or dialectical, explains the conversion of Paul, and that the enigma does not admit of a solution unless we acknowledge a miracle," Steinmeyer "The Passion and Resurrection History," p. 325.

For a striking example of the credulity of Strauss, and the outrageous suppositions of his impossible theory, see his account of Paul's conversion in his Life of Jesus.

[2] "In Paul we have a standard by which to measure the statements of the Gospels," Keim., p. 291.

leads Keim to the conclusion that Paul, like the other disciples, " sought the foundation of these actual occurrences (the appearances) in external instead of in internal spiritual facts."[1]

The vision theory, which we are not now concerned to discuss at length because our more immediate purpose is to examine an offshoot of it which has been grafted on to the Upas-tree of modern spiritualism, has been rejected by Keim himself. Not that Keim accepts the Christian belief. We have grown accustomed to the habits of sceptical critics. They are Herods who destroy every rival child to preserve their own. Keim rejects the vision theory of Strauss, because his own child is better fitted to survive. And he has reasons, he says, which are not "frequently heard upon the battlefield of the critics," which entirely overthrew the vision hypothesis.

The shells from the orthodox cannons, which have been hurled into the camp of the enemy, have done destructive work. As Christians we have urged, since the first appearance of this

[1] J. of N., vol. 6, p. 281.

popular explanation, that it is wholly inconsistent with the facts of the narrations, the sober character and limited number of the appearances, the depressed, hopeless state of mind and heart of the disciples, their blighted expectations, their unbelief in the Resurrection of Jesus although He told them He would rise again the third day, their confusion when the tomb was found empty, their doubts when their Master appeared to them, the sudden cessation of the appearances, the sober, earnest conduct of the disciples during the days which elapsed between the appearances and the day of Pentecost, and, most formidable of all the objections, the firm conviction of the disciples after the appearances, through ill repute and good, through trials and oppressions to the end and in the end, that Jesus Christ had Risen from the dead, and had been seen by them, and by hundreds of others still living when Paul wrote to the Corinthian Church.

Keim strengthens our objections in his deep-sighted criticism of the vision theory. His words, although many, must be quoted. "Visions were seen," he says— "so much remains certain according to Paul; but were they self-generated observations, that is, were they produced by the mere reverberation of the physically defunct spiritually immortal Jesus in the hearts and eyes of the believers? That is at once contradicted by the evidently simple, solemn, almost lifeless, cold, unfamiliar character of the manifestations. Only as the outcome of the strongest, of truly feverish excitement, as the outcome of the severest conflict of fervid faith and burning love with cold and terrible fate, could such self-generated visions be explained, and indeed they have been so explained. But this is contradicted by all the facts; from beginning to end there are only transient appearances, there are reserve and reticence in the face of the strange phenomenon; there is no trace of a happy, sweet, prolonged repose in the bosom of Him who is again endowed with life and love. The agitation that critics have assumed is invisible, or operates very imperfectly; and an appeal to the gulf generally made by death between the living and the departed, would be but the expedient of despair, since it would be full of contradiction. More glaring still becomes the inadequacy of the assumption when we glance at the orderly, regular, and early cessation of the appearances. The exuberance of excitement which generates ocular hallucinations demands a considerable length of time. The ebb does not immediately follow the flood, but is rather brought about by further excesses; one person excites another, and because the mental tension is continued, the appearances are repeated, occurring confessedly among the multitude, as every individual repeats what he has seen in his ecstasy, and every one of the twelve and every one of the five hundred demands afresh on his own behoof, and in his own mental experience, what he has first enjoyed in intercourse with others, and has derived from others. . . . . All this is false and frivolous with regard to the apostle's account. There was no hint of appearances, no exuberance, no indescribable irregularity, no violent transition. Certainly there were a few repetitions, since Peter, alive and with others, saw the Lord four times, the apostles saw him thrice, while on the other hand, the five hundred saw Him but once, and James once. Yet even these repetitions are no confirmation of the theory, but its refutation, because with the repetition of the self-generated vision, the facility, the tendency, the intensity, must grow far beyond the production of a fourfold or a three-fold vision.

"Still more damaging than the repetition is the end. Not one of the five hundred repeats the ecstasy, and all the cases of ecstasy irrevocably end with the fifth vision. What a contradiction of high-swollen enthusiasm, and of sudden ebb, even to the point of disappearance! Just when fervid minds are beginning to grow fanatical, the fanaticism absolutely and entirely ceases.

"Finally, the visions not only came to an end, they even made way for a diametrically opposite mental element. There lies before us the fact that the apostles passed at once from the visions to the clear recognition of the messianic dignity, of the heavenly glory of Jesus on the one hand, and to the definite and heroic resolve to bear witness for his cause on the other. All these considerations compel us to admit that the theory, which has recently become the favourite one, is only an hypothesis, which, while it explains something, leaves the main fact unexplained, and indeed subordinates what is historically attested to weak and untenable views."[1]

[1]The telegram theory which Keim adopts (J. of N., p. 323, 365,) is a mixture of the vision and the apparition theories. Prof. Milligan says in his curt reference to it, "it is unnecessary to discuss it at length . . . . it will satisfy no one."

The Apparition Theory.

The apparition theory, although it is an out-growth of spiritualism,[1] argues on the lines of the superstitious terror of the disciples who, when our Lord suddenly appeared in their midst, "supposed they had seen a spirit." It differs from the mythical theory of Strauss in a fundamental particular. Modern spiritualists do not regard the appearances of Jesus as hallucinations—visions created in the excited minds of the disciples without any external reality. The apparition theory assumes that Christ actually appeared, not in the body that was deposited in the rock tomb in the garden of Joseph of Arimathæa, but as a spirit form only. It likewise differs from the Christian conception in a fundamental principle. Spiritualists "look upon all spiritualistic phenomena as natural phenomena, and interpret scriptural and other miracles"[2] accordingly. We, as Christians, believe

[1]We are not here concerned to consider the reality of alleged modern apparitions; the apparition theory can be discussed without reference to them.
[2]Dr. Alfred Russell Wallace to the writer.

that the Resurrection was a supernatural event—
"God raised up" Jesus. Let us hear what this
offshoot of the vision theory, promulgated
assiduously in these latter days by spiritualists
who refuse to call themselves Christians, has to
say for itself.

The disappearance of the body and the
empty tomb is the rock upon which many
theories have been wrecked. Will the apparition
theory escape ? The advocates of the swoon
theory suggested that the stone was accidently or
intentionally removed by men (according to
Schleiermacher by the servants of the owner of
the garden, who knew nothing of the placing of
Jesus in the tomb, but only wished to bring the
stone back again to where it formerly stood in
order to let the air enter the newly-formed tomb),
and that Jesus crawled out half-alive. Other
theorists allege that Joseph secretly bore away the
body of Jesus " whilst it was yet dark," or that it
was not given to his friends for burial, but
was thrown into a pit with the two thieves.[1]
According to the apparition theory, the body was
" conveyed away " probably by some " spirit

[1] Strauss.

power " to a place where it was not discovered.[1]
Spiritualists do not contend that they have any
other warrant for this suggestion than the
necessity of accounting for the empty tomb.   It
certainly has no support from the only records we
possess. And the principle must be remembered, that
any theory which proposes to account for the belief
of the disciples in the Resurrection of Jesus Christ
must harmonize *all* the recorded facts of the four
Evangelists.   The rules of just criticism will not
allow any one to pick these statements to pieces by
tests derived from his own pre-conceptions.   But
the force of the principle is felt by our opponents,
inasmuch as they quote every fact which lends them
the least support.

Let us suppose, then, with the Spiritualists, that
the body of Christ is carried away and hid ; no one
need ask "how" or "why" because all answers can
only be guesses.   If He appears now it cannot well
be in the actual body which bore the imprint of the
nails.   There are a few items which are favourable
to this view.   First, "His not being recognised
when first seen by Mary."[2]   Now, when Mary and

[1]Dr. Wallace also Dr. Crowell in " Primitive Christianity
and Modern Spiritualism."
[2]Dr. Crowell.

the other women started from Bethany before the dawn they did not even think that they would find the tomb empty. As we read the Gospels the scenes of that Easter morning live before us. The sad belief that Christ is dead seems to be our belief. We are of the company of those loving disciples bearing the spices to anoint the sacred body and wondering who shall roll away for us the stone exceeding great. We enter the garden in the hush of early morning, softly treading upon the dewy grass and flowers, and, looking towards the tomb, we are struck as by a bolt from the blue. Our hands are involuntarily raised to our eyes, we strain forward; the stone is rolled aside, the tomb is open. We rush away with the women to call the disciples and run back with them to the garden. With the reverence of John we look into the tomb, and with the impetuosity of Peter enter boldly, see the grave clothes, but the body is gone. We wander about with Mary, distracted, and feel her hot tears upon our cheeks. We have come confident to find the body of Our Lord whom cruel hands maltreated; we are beside ourselves to find the body gone. Now the gardener approaches. We do not want him, we do not care to see a living man, we came to anoint the dead body of Our Loving Saviour. "They have taken away Our Lord and we know not where they have laid him," we cry in anguish. Now can anyone who reads this story with the sympathy always necessary to the discovery and appreciation of truth wonder that, for the moment, Mary did not recognise the living Christ? The fact that she mistook Him for the gardener is evidence in favour of her honest conviction that Jesus was dead. It cannot be fairly manufactured into a prop to support the apparition theory.

Another argument in favour of this view is drawn from the spiritual attributes of the body of Christ. " He could pass in and out of the closed doors, and appear and vanish instantaneously."[1] Whilst this is true, it is also true that he walked several miles, and ate and drank. The nature of the resurrection body is referred to on another page, but we may here remark that the object of Christ's appearances was to form a connection between His earthly life and His re-union with His Father ; and probably His body was accommodated to this mediate office. The main argument against the apparition theory is that it was distinctly overthrown by Christ himself.

[1]Referred to by Dr. Crowell.

"And as they spake these things He himself stood in the midst of them, and saith unto them, Peace be unto you.   But they were terrified and affrighted, and supposed that they beheld a spirit. And He said unto them, Why are ye troubled ? and wherefore do reasonings arise in your hearts? See my hands and my feet, that it is I myself, handle me and see ; for a spirit hath not flesh and bones as ye behold me having.   And when He had so said, He showed them his hands and his feet.   And while they still disbelieved for joy and wondered, He said unto them, Have ye here any-thing to eat ? And they gave him a piece of broiled fish.   And He took it and did eat before them."   (Luke xxiv. 36-43).

Against this it is argued that "Christ only here assured them that he came in a real body.   He did not even affirm that it was the same body that died on the cross."   (Dr. Wallace).   If Jesus Christ, in so many words, did not say "this is the same body that hung between the two thieves," he did lead them to believe it was (although transformed)[1] the

---

[1]Christlieb, remarks "it   was   the   same   body with the marks of the nails and the wound in its side, but in a new spiritual form of existence, and therefore standing under other laws."   Modern Doubt, p. 475.

very same body. Who would say that Our Lord did not intend Thomas to believe he was in the "same body" when he said to him, "Reach hither thy finger and see my hands and reach hither thy hand and thrust it into my side ; and be not faithless, but believing." (John xx, 27). Were the disciples deceived ? When He called her by name, Mary knew her Master's voice ; the two disciples at Emmaus recognised His familiar actions in the breaking of bread ; all the disciples who met at Galilee, and subsequently Thomas, identified His body. When the excitement of the first appearance had passed not one of them showed the least doubt of His identity. Did Jesus Christ deceive them ? It was a moral and physical impossibility. This apparition theory has not been propounded to destroy belief in the actual resurrection of Jesus Christ. The object of its author or authors has been to discover some support from the Life of Christ for modern spiritualistic phenomena.

About thirty years ago a theory like this apparition theory was born, and, as many supposed, quickly died. But Mrs. Besant contends that after the death and burial of our physical body, its astral corpse lingers about the churchyard and haunts the neighbourhood of its birth, and sometimes other neighbourhoods. These hazy forms are occasionally seen by ordinary folk, always by clairvoyants, and often in a state of decomposition. Theories, like men, must surely have an astral double.

THE THEORY OF CONSPIRACY.

The expectation that by arguments thrown apparently into syllogistic forms there is any compelling to the faith one who does not wish to believe is absurd and an expectation which all experience contradicts ; all that he is, and all that he is determined to be, has bribed him to an opposite conclusion. Rather than believe that a miracle has taken place, a miracle from the upper worlds, and connected with precepts of holiness, to which precepts he is resolved to yield no obedience, he will take refuge in any the most monstrous supposition of fraud, or ignorance, or folly, or collusion. (Trench on " Miracles," p. 96.)

V

THE THEORY OF CONSPIRACY.

" But truth will not allow herself to be tricked out by human
malice in the garb of falsehood."—DIDON.

THE theory of conspiracy[1] is propounded at length
in a book entitled " The Real Jesus : a review of
His life, character, and death, from a Jewish
standpoint," addressed to the Theistic church by
John Vickers.[2] The author considers that Jesus
Christ was a tool in the hands of several conspirators.

" He was no more an independent revelator than

[1] So far as I am aware, this theory, which I have called
the theory of conspiracy, has not been examined before. It
has been quoted by unbelievers, but never by a Christian
writer.

[2] As this book is addressed to the church of which the
Rev. Charles Voysey is the genial minister, we afforded him
the opportunity of expressing his general approval or disap-
proval of its contents. He writes :—" You have done me and
our church a real service by asking the question. We do
not agree with Mr. Vickers, and have regretted his great
departure from what we feel to be common sense. Our
theory implies no conscious insincerity or dishonesty, neither
on the part of Jesus nor on that of his followers."

His disciples were ; He was clearly instigated and moved by others, who would, of course, enjoin secrecy upon him ; His whole line of conduct affords evidence of His being a credulous zealot,[1] schooled by objective visions."[2]

The motive of the conspirators may be understood from this passage :—

" The Jews of that period who believed in the coming 'Kingdom of Heaven,' seem to have thought that with certain dramatic preparations and fulfilments of Scripture many others would be brought to believe, and that the predicted

[1] " The charge of an extravagant, self-deluding enthu-siasm is the last to be fastened on Jesus. Where can we find the traces of it in His history ? Do we detect them in the calm authority of his precepts, in the mild, practical, and beneficent spirit of his religion, in the unlaboured simplicity of the language with which He unfolds His high powers and sublime truths of religion, or in the good sense, the knowledge of human nature, which He always discovers in His estimate and treatment of the different classes of men with whom he acted ? Do we discover his enthusiasm in the singular fact that, whilst he claimed power in the future world, and always turned men's minds to Heaven, he never indulged His own imagination, or stimulated that of His disciples, by giving vivid pictures or any minute description of that unseen state ? The truth is that, remarkable as was the character of Jesus, it was distinguished by nothing more than by calmness and self-possession. This trait pervades his other excellencies. How calm was His piety ! Point me, if you can, to one vehement, passionate expression of his religious feelings. Does the Lord's Prayer breath a feverish enthu-

events would thus be accelerated. It was needful, in their estimation, that the suffering nation should have a suffering Messiah, who must die as a martyr and rise again in appearance foretokening the general resurrection. And it was not by mere persuasion and argument that a pious Galilean peasant would be led to believe that he was the Messiah[3] specially pointed to in Scripture and was required to undertake a mission which would involve the laying down of His life."[4]

Accordingly "the conspirators" seized upon Jesus to supply the dramatic fulfilments of Scripture.

The treatment of the Transfiguration may best

siasm ? His benevolence, too, though singularly earnest and deep, was composed and serene. He never lost the possession of Himself in His sympathy with others ; was never hurried into the impatient and rash enterprises of an enthusiastic philanthropy; but did good with the tranquility and constancy which mark the Providence of God." (Dr. Channing's " Discourse on the character of Christ," vol. iv., pp. 17, 18.)

[2]Vickers, p. 281.

[3]We might imagine a Jew of that age to have fancied Himself the Messiah and the Son of God ; but instead of opposing all the popular notions, and discouraging all the temporal hopes of his countrymen, he would, like Barcocheba of a later period, have headed a rebellion against the hated tyranny of the Romans, and endeavoured to establish a temporal kingdom. (Schaff, "The Person of Jesus," p. 105.)

[4]Vickers, p. 220.

introduce the working of this outrageous theory :—

"It seems to have been the object of those who appeared on the mountain in a spiritual guise not only to influence and instruct Jesus, but to furnish the chief disciples with very strong and impressive evidence that their Master had communion with the greatest of the prophets, and was really the divinely - commissioned Messiah. We are told that when Peter, James, and John had ascended the mountain to a distance, they were fatigued with the exertion and lay down to rest. While they were sleeping the 'Moses and Elias' of the drama whom Jesus would have been prepared to meet came forth from their concealment, and clothed him in a garment beautifully white. . . . The disciples were then awakened to witness with astonishment their Master thus gloriously robed, and the risen prophets who accompanied Him, while a voice from Heaven, which they supposed to be no other than God's voice, said : "This is my beloved Son, hear ye Him." The three disciples, like those initiated at the Greek mysteries, were naturally enough frightened at what they had seen and heard, and Jesus came at length and spoke to them familiarly and aroused them from their prostration. When they looked up they found their Master standing with them alone, so that they neither witnessed the advent nor the departure of the apparitions,[1] and came down from the mountain as fully confirmed in their faith, and as much enchanted with the foretaste of Paradise, as the devotees who in an interval of freedom from intoxicating stupor passed through the delightful gardens of Alimoot."[2]

Let us watch how the author handles the Crucifixion. The conspirators persuaded Jesus that if He submitted to death He would rise again in three days.

"The real heads of the sect, Joseph of Arimathea and others, who had secret intercourse with Him, had an obvious reason for predicting this (His rising again in three days), as though it had been revealed from Heaven that He might the more readily devote Himself to martyrdom, and his disciples be the more disposed at the appointed time to believe in the projected miracle of the Resurrection."

[1] Conspirators is meant.
[2] Vickers, p. 220 and 221.

Having encouraged Jesus to suffer death, strengthened by the belief that He was "fulfilling Scripture texts," and would rise again, they set about arranging the Crucifixion.

"There can be little doubt that the same secret chiefs of the Nazarene sect, who got up the mountain vision and spoke of the martyrdom which he was soon to suffer, were really instrumental to its accomplishment. They had, under the guise of messengers from Heaven, directed their Messianic devotee to go up to Jerusalem, and there to die, to rise again according to the Scriptures, and now they had arrived within the city they laboured craftily and assiduously for the completion of their design."

"It was to them simply the getting up of a masked drama to impose on the world ; they stood behind the scenes and commanded the whole of the movements ; they had only to engage a number of people to act certain parts to do this, that, and the other thing, for a small payment, as they directed, and the religious mystery was performed with entire success. Those who crucified Jesus, mocked and insulted Him, no more acted from natural impulse than do their modern imitators in the Bavarian Passion Play.[1] They did as they were told, just to fulfil Scripture and produce a strong impression on the minds of the spectators ; the whole story is dramatic, coloured to some little extent with mythical embellishments."[2]

We are now prepared to witness the theory of conspiracy applied to the Resurrection. The conspirators, of course, obtained the body of Jesus. They " had the placing of the Roman watch at the sepulchre . . . and it was a prudent and well-arranged measure."

" It might naturally seem advisable to them, under these circumstances, to place a guard at the sepulchre to keep away all impertinent and hostile intruders. And who could be more fitted

---

[1]This is an unwarrantable reflection upon the pious peasants of Ober Ammergau. " The performance of the Passion Play, like the angel with the drawn sword which stands on the summit of the castle of San Angelo, is the pious recognition of a miraculous interposition for the stay of pestilence, a kind of dramatic rainbow set in the hills to commemorate the stay of the pestilential deluge." Waisenbergh, the parish priest of Ober Ammergau, wrote that he "undertook the production of the play for the love of my Divine Redeemer, and with only one object in view, the edification of the Christian world." (Mr. Stead writing home from Ober Ammergau, June 9th, 1890).

[2]Vickers, p. 238.

for such a task than their late hired assistants, the Roman soldiers, who had so well acted their part of fulfilling prophecy at the Crucifixion? Moreover, by getting a military guard placed at the tomb for the ostensible purpose of preventing the expected fraudulent resurrection, it might tend to lull suspicion, to quiet and satisfy those who were really apprehensive of a secret abstraction of the body, and who might otherwise have deemed it necessary to be present and watch for themselves."[1]

The Roman watch obeyed the orders of the conspirators, and dispersed into the city, when the latter arrived "whilst it was dark," and "secretly bore away the body." Jesus is now dead, and His body will not again be seen by friend or foe. How, then, did the conspirators carry out their object? First, they stationed "some of their party at the sepulchre when the body was abstracted to start the report that Jesus had actually risen from the dead, and was gone into Galilee to the place where he had appointed to meet them."

Then—

"They would not think of carrying off and

[1] Vickers, p. 242.

concealing the dead prophet of Nazareth without providing a living representative to go forth in his place and fulfil the prediction of his rising. In order to complete their resurrection drama it would be necessary for one of the confederacy to personate[1] the revived Jesus before some of the leading disciples, as they had on a former occasion personated Moses and Elias in Galilee. Accordingly, we find in the Gospel narrative an account of a mysterious[2] visitor presenting himself to a few[3] privileged beholders in that character. It is generally supposed that this person, who obtruded himself on the notice of the disciples occasionally, soon after the evacuation of the sepulchre, was believed by them to be Jesus, on the ground of his perfect identity in

---

[1]Could a conspirator personate Jesus, "who stood in the first rank of the grand family of the true Sons of God " (Renan). "The chosen of God, His image, His darling, His world-guide and world-shaper in the history of mankind " (Keim). " The well-spring of whatever is best and purest in Christian life " (Lecky). " The regenerator of humanity " (Francis Power Cobbe) ?

[2]He was recognised by all. But if the belief in the Resurrection arose from a case of personation, a close examination by those who knew him would lead to detection, not recognition.

[3]I. Cor. xv. 6.

form and feature with their late Master."[1]

The disciples believed in "this living representative" because

"they were fully prepared and confidently
looking[2] for their revived Master before anyone
in that character made his appearance. They
probably did not at first expect to meet Him
until they had arrived at the mountain in
Galilee ; but when they found that the sepulchre
was empty, heard that He was risen, and that He
had been seen alive in the neighbourhood, their
minds would not fail to become excited, and their
eyes would have been ready to anticipate His
appearance in the form of every stranger[3] who
approached them.   When, therefore, a personator
of Jesus did actually present Himself, a few weak[4]
circumstantial evidences that He was armed with
sufficed to convince them of his identity."[1]

As soon as the two who went to Emmaus
recognised "the living representative, He vanished
out of their sight."   The crucifixion wounds "are

[1]Vickers, p. 247.
[2]St. John xx. 9.
[3]This is inconsistent with Matt. xxviii. 17.
[4]Luke xxiv. 39.   John xx. 27.
[1]Vickers, p. 251.

a mythical embellishment by the Gospel writers."
So also, in the author's opinion, is every particle of
evidence that can be found in the Gospels against
this theory of conspiracy ; and it should be cut out.
If any difficulties remain after this judicious appli-
cation of the scissors—well, he writes :—"It is by
no means rare for men to lie, both consciously and
unconsciously, in agreement with their passions and
their apparent interest."

" Where is the actual resurrection ? It seems
to have been much such a miracle as the trans-
mutation which now takes place occasionally
under the box of the conjuror ; the people who
stand as spectators are permitted to see the dead
thing which goes in, and the live thing which
comes out, and having these few intimations and
suggestions of a miracle given them, are expected
to imagine and believe the rest."

The Ascension was worked on the same prin-
ciples as the Transfiguration trick :—

" While they stood gazing into the skies, 'two
men, in white apparel,' who might have been
' Moses and Elias,' or the ' angels' who had
recently been posted at the sepulchre, suddenly
approached and persuaded them to cease gazing,

as Jesus had flown away beyond their sight, but would at some future time so come from Heaven and visit them again."[1]

I have given this theory in the language of its originator. There are some theories and objections which are so malicious and absurd that it is only necessary to state them in order to ensure their rejection by every just thinker. In the first rank of these stands this theory of conspiracy. To state it in its nakedness is to refute and condemn it, and to cover its author with shame. It is impossible to seriously discuss it. It is simply a clumsy effort of his imagination. His conspirators are surely the vilest of their vile race. Can light be born of Egyptian darkness? He has not hesitated to make them lie in the name and to the face of God in whom they are supposed to believe. Could hypocrites establish an honest religion that should live two thousand years and have the promise of eternal life? To suggest that they were prompted by a desire to fulfil Scripture is without doubt to make them madmen. And who could recognise the Apostles among the band of dupes humbugged by such transparent trickery? Was John a double-

[1]Vickers, p. 260.

dyed Judas? Was Paul only Saul in lamb's clothing? Renan, in his illusory style, says that Mary in a moment of divine intoxication started the story that Christ had risen from the dead. But Mr. Vickers stations a party at the tomb, who, for pay, boldly lied "to fulfil Scripture," and declared, "He is risen." The Jesus of Renan's romance is "at the highest summit of human greatness," "his great originality remains undiminished; his glory admits no legitimate sharer." "From the midst of uniform mediocrity there are pillars that rise towards the sky. Jesus is the highest of these pillars. In him was condensed all that is good and elevated in our nature," "between him and God men will no longer distinguish."[1] But the Jesus of the conspiracy occupies a much lower place.

"Some of the more thoughtful may now and then in their closets feel assured that the modern Church has produced men greatly superior in every way to the rude Galilean preacher who serves as its figure head."[2]

Yet these thoughtful disciples—

[1]L. of J., p. 291
[2]Vickers.

" Would on no account venture to hint this to the idolatrous multitude . . . . they make the best of him as a moral exemplar by ascribing to him their own virtues and every other excellence recognized in Christendom."[1]

It is surpassing strange that the courageous author, who certainly does not fear the idolatrous multitude, does not mention one modern man greatly superior in every way to the rude Galilean preacher. Why not ? Evidently, he is bent upon making all men hypocrites to suit the requirements of his theory. Verily, he has crucified the Son of God afresh and put Him to an open shame. This "real Jesus " is a dupe—nay, God forgive us for even writing the blasphemy —worse than a dupe— a veritable fool. Is this the Jesus for whom the Protomartyr submitted to be stoned to death ? And of whom the aged Polycarp, who sat at the feet of His beloved disciple, exclaimed, as the furious mob piled the fagots about Him and wished to nail him to the stake—" He that giveth me strength to endure the fire will also enable me, without securing me by nails, to remain without moving in

[1]Vickers, p. 5.

the pile " ?[1]   Did this " Real Jesus " inspire such magnificent courage ?   Did Blandina, the Christian slave, whose martyrdom is the most pathetic and the bravest of all the thousands who loved Jesus even unto death, bear the fury of the wild beasts and the horrors of the white-hot chair for this fool? Did this "Real Jesus " found the Christian Church which overthrew the Pagan philosophies and revolutionised the Roman Empire and " who each day still presides over the destiny of the world " ? Is this the Jesus whose sublime thoughts have lifted us above all meanness and trickery and inspired us to lead better lives ?   Is this the Jesus " whose history will provoke endless tears, whose sufferings will subdue the stoutest hearts," who is the Author of the " Sermon on the Mount," which Renan declares " will never be surpassed " ? Is this the Jesus whom his enemies admire ?   Is this the Saviour of our lives—Our Lord and our God ? The theory of conspiracy is not in moral unity with the undoubted influence of Christ upon the world. This " Real Jesus " is a mental and moral impossibility. Why has the author made Jesus, His Disciples and His followers in all ages foolish

[1]See the circular Epistle of the Church of Smyrna.

impostors ? Why ? The moral responsibility of this hideous misuse of the artless records of the four Evangelists is beyond reckoning. We shut the covers of the " Real Jesus " in profound sorrow and shame, and beg the author and his followers to compare their made-up pitiable figure with the pure, noble, tender man whose image is stamped on every scene of the Gospels, but on none more deeply than on this scene of infinite mercy.

WHEN THEY WERE COME TO THE PLACE WHICH IS CALLED CALVARY; THERE THEY CRUCIFIED HIM AND THE MALEFACTORS; ONE ON THE RIGHT HAND, AND THE OTHER ON THE LEFT.

THEN JESUS SAID, "FATHER, FORGIVE THEM, FOR THEY KNOW NOT WHAT THEY DO."

A FEW THEORETICAL OBJECTIONS.

VI

A FEW THEORETICAL OBJECTIONS.

In Great Britain and America pamphlets have been very widely circulated, in which freethinkers criticise the testimonies of Matthew, Mark, Luke, John and Paul, without committing themselves to any theory to account for the belief of the Apostles in the Resurrection of the Messiah. We have elsewhere said that this attitude is not just. Either Christ did or did not rise from the dead : if the critic believes in his own heart that He did not, he ought either (*a*) to state and defend his own belief, or (*b*) to account for our belief that he did. These critics, however, rejoice in the work of destruction. Let us read, in their own language, some of their objections.

(*A*). " If Jesus had died on the cross, how could He have exhibited Himself to his disciples as a living man, and especially have directed their

attention to His body, in reality, flesh and
blood ? " " Reach hither thy finger," said Jesus,
" and behold my hands ; and reach hither thy
hand and thrust it into my side, and be not
faithless but believing." (John xx., 27).

" Here is Jesus presenting Himself for the
express purpose of demonstrating to the senses
of His friends that He was no phantom, no spirit,
no shadow ; but a solid and living body, that
might be seen and touched, and felt. Now, if
the body were solid, and could be seen and felt,
and required nourishment to support it, then is
the account that Jesus had really been " crucified, dead and buried," a fiction by evidence as
strong as ever was adduced, namely, the evidence of Jesus Himself." *The true source of
Christianity*, by an Indian Officer, pp. 113—114.

This is truly a strange objection. Jesus Christ
shewed himself alive after his reported resurrection, therefore he did not die, therefore he did not
rise from the dead. The writer here considers it a
fact that Jesus was alive after his supposed death.
Strauss is sure that Jesus Christ died ; he says
" the account of the evangelists about the death of

Jesus is in itself connected, clear, and unanimous."[1] It would therefore seem, that being given an Indian Officer and Strauss as witnesses, Christ must have risen from the dead. We rejoice because we have the evidence of Christ himself, "that he was a solid body, and could be seen and felt." But if his evidence *is* acceptable,[2] did he not declare that he would die and rise again from the dead ? Did he not distinctly cause the disciples to believe in his Resurrection from the dead?

(*B*). Again the same writer, thoroughly typical of the class who compose atheistic pamphlets to scatter broadcast among working men, says :—

"The Gospel writers fell into sad error in narrating this event by acknowledging that the seal was broken, and the stone which covered the mouth of the sepulchre removed ; for if they had intended a real miracle and a true resurrection, they ought to have left the seal and the stone untouched, and yet the body gone ; therein would have consisted the real miracle. The

[1]See also Schenkel.

[2]" We must take the history as it is, or deny it as a whole. To take away all in it that is transcendent and miraculous, is to destroy it, not in itself, for it defies destruction, but in the minds of those who try to purify it, as they say, from its supernatural element." (Didon. Jesus Christ, p. 72).

very fact of it being necessary to break the seal, and remove the stone for the purpose of liberating the body of Jesus would show that human and not divine means had been employed in effecting this object, and thus have exposed its fictitious character."[1]

Once more the assumption that the Gospel writers composed their narrative with the deliberate purpose of imposing upon the reader, lurks behind this objection.

They made no mistake in stating what they knew to be true. They had no theory to maintain, and therefore had no need to surround the Resurrection with unnecessary marvels.[2] A writer of fiction might do so, but the Evangelists declare that "which we have heard, which we have seen with our eyes, which we have looked upon, and our hands have handled, of the Word of Life" (1 John, i., 1.) Would our critic or any other objector have believed in the resurrection if

[1] Page 3.
[2] Luke xi., 29; Matt. xvi., 1; John iv., 48.

Christ had passed through the tombstone and left the seal unbroken? Assuredly not.[1] And why could human hands alone have broken the seal and rolled back the stone? Is there no other superior power in the universe? Matthew says "an angel of the Lord had descended from heaven and came and rolled back the stone." Does our critic start with another assumption that the supernatural does not exist? Assuredly yes: this is why a "human conspirator" is introduced to take the place of the Angel.

(C). Another sceptic to whom we have referred at length, says:—

"If the crucified Jesus had actually risen from the dead, his wounds, which were the cause of his death, must certainly have been healed, so that he would have come forth from the tomb perfectly whole. When a person now and then comes forward professing to be the lost heir of an estate, any scars or tattooings which he may have exhibited for the purpose of identification are invariably regarded by shrewd magistrates with the greatest mistrust. Yet it is precisely on evidence of this kind, exhibited nearly two

[1]Luke xvi., 31.

thousand years ago, that we are now expected to believe in the supernatural origin of Christianity."[1]

Is it not a sufficient answer to say, that, in the Providence of God, these wounds were visible in the risen body of Jesus Christ for the benefit of all, who, like Thomas, sweep aside the testimony of other witnesses as unconvincing and trust no one but themselves? To all who see themselves in this exacting Apostle, Our Lord says:— " Thomas——blessed are they that have not seen and yet have believed." Apart from this consideration, the possibility of Christ's walking about with the wounds of the nails and spear does not enter into the question, "Did he rise from the dead?" Because (a), if he arose from the dead, he could surely overcome this minor obstacle to locomotion : (b), if he did not rise, the detail is not worth considering.

The nature of our Lord's body between His Resurrection and His Ascension will never be perfectly understood by us.

" The body, which He had given up to all the suffering and torments of crucifixion, is now for

[1] " The Real Jesus," p. 253.

ever freed from the laws of suffering and corruption. It cannot change, it cannot suffer. It acquires a sort of spirituality. Matter with its grossness and denseness troubles it no more, it is possessed of a subtlety which can penetrate matter. It is no longer controlled by laws of gravitation, no longer limited by space; it is as swift and agile as the will which moves it, and whose perfect instrument it is. It becomes palpable and visible at pleasure; it appears and disappears as it chooses. As the soul assumes the form of its ideas so the body of Jesus assumes the form which best becomes it, without interfering with the essentials of its nature and identity. Yet it has retained its wounds to be the glorious and ineffaceable marks of its earthly struggles, and even in his Heavenly Kingdom to witness to his victory over sin, and his infinite love towards mankind."[1]

If the reference to the lost heir of an estate be intended as an analogy, it does not hold in any particular: neither is it a fair illustration of the way in which magistrates regard scars as a means of identification. It would be nearer the truth to say,—If it were a question of the identification of

[1]Didon. " Jesus Christ."

a body, magistrates, friends, and enemies alike would pay the strictest regard to such unmistakable scars as those produced by crucifixion ; and it is the general practice of the police to show great attention to the marks upon the bodies of prisoners, because they have often cleared up the mystery of a murder, and considerably shaped a verdict by such evidence.

The last clause, " Yet it is precisely on evidence of this kind, exhibited nearly two thousand years ago, that we are now expected to believe in the supernatural origin of Christianity " is illogical and untrue. The supernatural origin of Christianity does not rest upon the single fact that Our Lord exhibited His wounds in proof that He was the same being risen from the dead. The Christian evidences are cumulative, and embrace very numerous lines of independent evidence.

(D). A more plausible objection is contained in the following questions :—(a) " Why did Christ first appear to Mary and the other women upon whose assertion the resurrection mainly rests ? " (b) " When His taking one turn in the public market place or the temple would have been the greatest of miracles, and would have spared the painful labours and lives of so many vouchers who perished merely by these things being done in a corner?"[1]

We may remark, (*a*) It has been truly and beautifully said, and it is an all sufficient answer to this part of the question, " that no one was worthier than the Magdalene to be the first to see Jesus." But the Resurrection does not rest mainly on the assertions of women. " He was seen of Cephas, then of the twelve, after that he was seen of above 500 brethren at once; of whom the greater part remain unto this present, but some are fallen asleep. After that he was seen of James; then of the apostles. And last of all he was seen of me also as of one born out of due time."[2]   (1, Cor. xv., 5—8).

(*b*) This is loose reasoning; his taking one turn in the public market would not have been in itself " the greatest of miracles "; it would not have been a miracle at all. Now Peter declared

[1] Even Dr. Martineau makes much of this shallow objection. He says " It is impossible to account for his having never appeared to the enemies and blind multitude who most needed to be convinced." " Seat of Authority," p. 374.

[2] For popular arguments in favour of the authenticity of St. Paul's Epistles, see Present Day Tracts (Published by the Religious Tract Society).

the purpose of God in the appearances of the Risen Saviour when he said—

"Him God raised up the third day, and gave him to be made manifest, not to all the people, but unto witnesses that were chosen before God." (Acts x., 41.)

Every critic is able to tell Jesus Christ what he ought to have done to satisfy criticism. May we not also say with truth that had he appeared before his enemies who cried, "Crucify Him, Crucify Him," they would not have believed, for even Martineau says they were "blind." It is certain that an additional appearance before His enemies would not have convinced the critic who is unsatisfied with the appearances detailed by Paul, and the fact that within forty days after Christ's death the witnesses to His resurrection published His name abroad before these very people, and ultimately gave their lives to uphold the truth of their declaration. But if the gospels be the work of pious writers bent upon proving that Christ arose from the dead, how is it they have not created such an appearance ? " Had they aimed to make the testimony as strong as possible without regard to truth, they would have represented Him as appearing also to His opponents."[1] Such an appearance, however, would have been so inconsistent with the purposes of Christ that, " Had it been told us that Christ did, as Schenkel would have had him, *made a public show of himself* before his enemies, then we should have great reasons to doubt the veracity of the records which contained such a statement. That he did not do so speaks for the credibility of His reappearances."[2] Behind this demand for an appearance before His enemies[3] is the lack of belief in the supernatural. These theoretical objections are atheistic.

(E). A more trifling objection is the following, taken from a tract written by a leading spiritualist (editor of a newspaper), and published quite recently.

" Where was Jesus crucified ? Matthew, Mark,

---

[1]Neander
[2]Christlieb.
[3]" The manifestation of a risen Saviour was only designed for those who had been brought to faith by his previous ministry. It was not one of the miracles by which unbelievers were to be convinced. Those whose disposition of heart had made them unsusceptible of impression from his whole ministry would have received, for the same reason, but transient impressions from his reappearance. If the living Christ could not lead them to repent, neither would they have been persuaded by one risen from the dead." Neander—" Life of Christ," p. 475.

and John say at Golgotha, but Luke says it was Calvary. Which was it, either or neither ? "

Like the theory of conspiracy this question requires no answer.

(*F*). From the same source is this :—

" Then the eleven went into Galilee, where they should see Him. "But some doubted." Most significant that " some doubted." If they doubted who were witnesses, how can we reasonably believe ? "[1]

Sometimes unbelievers allege that the disciples were ready to see the risen Jesus in every stranger. Against this allegation it is useful to refer to the fact " some doubted." They asked, if not openly like Thomas, then in their minds, for evidence. This is the meaning of the doubts. But their doubts were removed, and each of them came to recognise Jesus as the Risen Saviour. We can " reasonably believe" because the disciples did not continue to doubt, but were satisfied, and afterwards suffered death for their convictions. Ought not this to have been mentioned in this objection ?

---

[1] " Did Jesus Die on the Cross," by E. W. Wallis, p. 57.
See also Martineau, p. 372, who, however says, " this expression of objective uncertainty favours the idea of something visionary in the manifestation."

(*G*). Some time ago the following subject was introduced to a public audience, by a well-known atheist,
in a statement against the evidence of Paul for the
resurrection of Jesus Christ. "St. Paul made a
mistake," said the speaker, "which discredits his
testimony. In Cor. xv., 6th ver., he says, "Christ
appeared to the twelve." Now we are certain
Judas was not there, and it is generally agreed
Thomas was absent—therefore he did not appear
to the twelve."

The answer to this is simple. The words "The
Twelve" are used by Paul as a sort of generic name
or title indicating the whole body, as one body, of
the apostles. In politics we have a political body
called "The Liberal Hundred," but if only ninety-
eight of them met, and it was reported "The
Liberal Hundred met last evening," no one would
reasonably find fault with the statement. Paul
made no mistake. "The Twelve" is evidently a
technical and customary title for "The Apostles,"
and was used irrespective of the actual number
present. The Rev. Teignmouth Shore once told
the present writer that he remembered saying in a
sermon, "Then he appeared to 'The Twelve,' Thomas
being absent," and no one was so absurdly captious

as to suggest he ought to have said " The Ten."

(*H*). Every objector discovers the following contradiction :—

According to St. Mark, "the women went to the tomb when the sun was risen." According to St. John, "early when it was yet dark." "How shall I meet this terrible difficulty ? " says Lacordaire : " It suffices to comprehend that when a distance is to be reached early in the morning, it is possible to start before sunrise and arrive at daybreak." Most of these difficulties, of which the above are a fair specimen, are supplied from the larder of Strauss, and lavishly spread before the reader of these modern pamphlets.

" I have read Strauss' work with attention and labour, and I did so in this manner. After having studied a paragraph, always a very long one, and there are 149 of them filling 4 volumes, I closed the book to recover a little from the fatigue and from a kind of involuntary terror caused by the abundance of erudition. Then opening the gospel—which I kissed respectfully—I read the texts under discussion to see if by the simple aid of ordinary literature, and without the help of any commentators I could not succeed in unravelling the difficulty. With the

exception of three or four passages I have never required more than ten minutes to dissipate the charm
of vain knowledge, and to smile within myself at
the powerlessness to which God has condemned
error."[1]

We have seen that the critics examine the
Resurrection with the preconceived notion that
Christ could *not* rise from the dead. May we not
be fully justified in holding it was not possible that
Christ should be holden of death, as Peter boldly
declared in Jerusalem a few weeks after the ascension ? Death was the curse pronounced upon man
as a consequence of sin. But Jesus was sinless,[2]
and the Prince of Life ; how could he die ? " No
man taketh My life from Me but I lay it down of
Myself. 1 have power to lay it down, and I have
power to take it up again."

[1] " Jesus Christ, God, God and Man," p. 130. [2]John viii., 46.
[2] " To those who seem to understand only the laws of
physical and animal nature it is well to recall the universal
laws of nature, moral and human, rational and divine. Death
is the logical, fatal inexorable consequence of sin. And if any
being has remained untainted by sin, it is just that he should
escape death. The absolute holiness of Jesus guarded Him
against dissolution, and if, in His love towards men, Jesus
delivered Himself np to death, of His own free will, and in
accordance with the commandment of His Father, the justice
of God was to deliver Him from it for ever. The Resurrection
is the great act of divine justice towards the only innocent
being that the world has ever known." (Didon, Jesus Christ,
p. 380).

CONCLUSION.

The transition from the theories we have been considering to the record of the four Evangelists is like passing out of a stifling yellow fog to the clear light and bracing air of a spring morning. To turn from the Jesus of visions and dramas to the Jesus of the Gospels is like turning from a deceptive marsh light to face the full glory of the sun. " But are there not differences between the four accounts," asks the sceptic? Yes; because each writes to reveal a, different aspect of Jesus Christ,[1] and sometimes of the self-same facts. To St. Matthew, Jesus Christ is the Son of Abraham and David; to St. Mark, the Apostle's servant, He is a servant; to St. Luke, the physician, He is the Saviour of the ruined and the lost; to St. John, who leaned upon His Master's breast, Jesus is the Eternal Son who was in the bosom of the Father. All do not speak directly of His miraculous

[1]Westcott's Introduction.

birth, nor of His baptism, nor of His fasting, nor of His transfiguration. But there is a divine unity underlying these differences and omissions; and the Gospels can only be opposed to each other by violent interpretations.

" We see and feel that St. Matthew, St. Mark, St. Luke, St. John are different souls, and that each traces in his own manner, the likeness of his beloved Master, without taking the least account of what his neighbour is doing, or even of what the continuity of chronology requires. Hence an arbitary choice of fragments, a default of connection, apparent contradiction, details omitted by one and related by another, a multitude of varieties of which men render no account to themselves. This is true. And yet in these four evangelists there is the same portraiture of Christ, the same sublimity, the same tenderness, the same force, the same language, the same accent, the same supreme singularity of physiognomy.

" Open St. Matthew the publican, or St. John the young man, chaste and contemplative; choose whatever passage you will in the one or in the other, different alike in matter and in expression, and speak it before a thousand men assembled together, all will raise their heads; they recognise Jesus Christ. And the more the exterior disagreement of the Gospel is shown, the more the intimate agreement whence the moral unity of Christ springs will become a proof of their fidelity. If they unanimously represent so well the inimitable features of Christ, it is because He was before their eyes; they saw Him such as He was and such as they were not able to forget Him. They saw Him with their senses, with their hearts, with the exactitude of a love which was to give its blood; they are at the same time witnesses, painters and martyrs. That sitting of God before man has been witnessed only once, and this is why there is but one Gospel, although there were four evangelists."[1]

Yet, as if to meet the cold, heartless demands ot the intellect alone respecting the central fact of our faith, the Evangelists are unanimous in their testimony to the Death and Resurrection of the Christ, the Son of the Living God. All the writers declare that the Sanhedrim consulted to take Jesus by subtlety; all, that Judas betrayed his Master,

[1]Lacordaire. " Jesus Christ," p. 132.

and that He was arrested in the garden of agony; all, that He was brought before Caiphas and owned His Messiahship and Godhead, and was condemned for blasphemy and mocked; all, that He was brought before Pilate and scourged; all, that the Jews shouted for His blood, and that He was delivered up to be crucified; all, that He was crucified at Golgotha, and gave up the ghost; all, that the body was taken down from the cross and buried in the tomb of Joseph of Arimathæa; all, that the women and the disciples found the sepulchre open and the body gone on the first Easter Sunday; all, that He arose, and as the Risen Saviour appeared to the twelve disciples and to many others.

This is the Christian theory of the Trial, Death, and Resurrection of Jesus Christ in the combined testimonies of the Evangelists, which we accept as the reasonable solution of all doubts.

THE END.